Hotel & Restaurant Design No.3

Roger Yee

THE MANY MOODS OF METAL.

Chemetal crushed it at Fashion Week. Hundreds of sheets of Polished Aluminum decorated this runway set. Chemetal has hundreds of metal designs for your next project. Full story at chemetal.com

CHEMETAL

Hotel & Restaurant Design No.3

302 Fifth Avenue • New York, NY 10001
Tel: 212.279.7000 • Fax: 212.279.7014

www.visualreference.com

PUBLISHER — Larry Fuersich
larry@visualreference.com

EDITORIAL DIRECTOR — Roger Yee
rhtyee@gmail.com

CREATIVE ART DIRECTOR — Martina Parisi
martina@visualreference.com

PRODUCTION MANAGER — John Hogan
johnhvrp@yahoo.com

BUSINESS MANAGER — Angie Goulimis
angie@visualreference.com

Library of Congress Cataloging in Publication Data: Hotel & Restaurant Design No.3

ISBN 13: 978-0-9825989-5-5
ISBN 10: 0-9825989-5-5

Distributors to the trade in the United States and Canada
Innovative Logistics
575 Prospect Street
Lakewood, NJ 08701
732.363.5679

Distributors outside the United States and Canada
HarperCollins International
10 East 53rd Street
New York, NY 10022-5299

Exclusive distributor in China
Beijing Designerbooks Co., Ltd.
B-0619, No.2 Building, Dacheng International Center
78 East 4th Ring Middle Road
Chaoyang District, Beijing 100022, P.R. China
Tel: 0086(010)5962-6195 Fax: 0086(010)5962-6193
E-mail: info@designerbooks.net www.designerbooks.net

Printed and bound in China

Book Design: Martina Parisi

The paper on which this book is printed contains recycled content to support a sustainable world.

Hotel & Restaurant Design No.3

Roger Yee

Visual Profile Books Inc., New York

Contents

Sleepers—and Diners—Awake!

By Roger Yee

Where do you want to go today? Downtown for dinner and a show? Walt Disney World with the children or grandchildren? Overseas to the glories of London, Paris and Rome—or maybe something more exotic this time? Good times and bad, Americans respond to the same restless urge that has lured such noted travelers as Daniel Boone, Herman Melville and Jack Kerouac out of the house and on the road (or high seas). Now that the economic recovery is finally gaining momentum, business travelers are back in force, and leisure travelers are beginning to follow them. For architects and interior designers serving the hospitality industry, the return of projects for renovation and new construction could not come soon enough.

Suddenly travelers are learning it pays to book hotel accommodations early again. Occupancy rates have risen by nearly six percent in 2010 from 54.7 percent in 2009 and the volume of meetings is expected to grow by eight percent in 2011. Little new construction is looming to alleviate the surge, thanks to financial markets with little appetite for commercial real estate development and even less for new hotels, domestic innkeepers are even contemplating hikes in room rates for the 4.76 million guestrooms they now offer in properties with 15 or more rooms. Meanwhile, they are busying themselves with renovations and additions to differentiate their properties, build brand equity and keep quality high—while exploiting fresh opportunities abroad, where hotel design and construction are racing to stay abreast of demand, especially in developing countries.

Two out of five consumers say they are not dining out as often as they would like, setting an upbeat tone for the restaurant

Pool at Capella Pedregal Cabo San Lucas in Cabo San Lucas BCS, Mexico. Designed by HKS Hill Glazier Studio. Photography byRichard Holland/Robert Reck Photography.

industry's anticipated revenue growth in 2011, following three years of declining sales. Sales are projected to advance 3.6 percent in 2011 over 2010 sales, a 1.1 percent increase in inflation-adjusted terms. The return of patrons will not catch operators of the nation's 960,000 restaurants by surprise. Displaying resourcefulness and creativity in sustaining the population's love of dining out, restaurateurs have kept entrées affordable, acknowledged environmental and health issues, and enhanced the overall dining experience as a leisure activity. Now that everyone, and not just restaurant reviewers, Zagat, Mobil and Michelin, is expressing effusive and often colorful opinions about food, service and décor—complete with photography—via social media and online

review sites such as Yelp and Chowhound, restaurateurs are taking online commentary very seriously.

All of this makes design more important than ever to the hospitality industry. As the following pages of exceptional new hotels and restaurants show, leading architects and interior designers are working closely with hoteliers and restaurateurs to give consumers more delectable reasons to travel and dine out. Too good to be true? Why not hit the road today, and find out for yourself?

Roger Yee
Editor

THE ROGER THOMAS COLLECTION

Design: Tuileries
Hand Tufted Wool Carpet

Wynn Encore Macau

The Natural Carpet Company

OMBRE
Design Rockwell Group

OMBRE S

OMBRE PP

OMBRE PP SATINATO

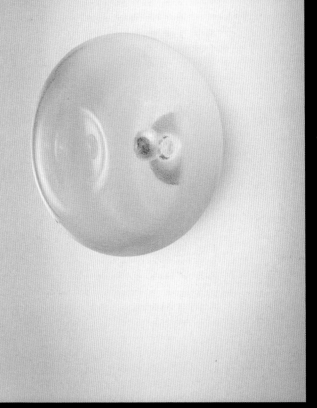

OMBRE PP 35 and 45
Application for wall or ceiling.
Blown from amber smoked glass
infused with silica sand dust.
Offered in two sizes.
Also available for compact fluorescent lamping.
Metal structure finish in brushed bronze.

OMBRE S
Teardrop pendant blown from amber
smoked glass diffuser infused with silica
sand dust. Metal structure and canopy
finish in brushed bronze. Optional swag.

LEUCOS USA INC. - 11 MAYFIELD AVENUE, EDISON, N.J. 08837 - Tel. (732) 225-0010 - info@leucosusa.com - www.leucos.com

LEUCOS

ANN KALE

1569 San Leandro Lane • Santa Barbara, CA 93108 • 805.969.7660 • 805.969.7663 (Fax)

www.annkale.com

ANN KALE ASSOCIATES   Lucier | Portland, Oregon

Restaurateurs have their dreams much as other entrepreneurs, and the developers of Lucier, a restaurant in Portland's South Waterfront neighborhood, have aimed high. As co-owner Chris Dussin, whose family operates the popular Old Spaghetti Factory chain, told *The Oregonian,* "We want this to be the ultimate dining destination in Portland." Interiors designed by Alvarez + Brock with lighting design by Ann Kale Associates, stands 10 feet from the Willamette River. Expressive inside and outside, the 6,700-square- foot space suavely complements

Lucier's contemporary European cuisine. Its 240-foot-long by 20-foot-high glass walls capture river views and sunshine by day. After sundown, the contrast between the dining room, an expansive volume through which a water channel meanders, and the bar, a compact space dominated by a large community bar, is heightened by lighting. The dining room chandeliers, bronze rods suspended in a spiral pattern around a central glass fixture, cast a soft glow accented by dancing light waves from spotlights on the water channel. More intimate and seductive,

the bar enlists recessed lights, rope lighting from below, custom floor lamps and illuminated cocktail tables. The setting—plus chef Pascal Chureau's cuisine—earned Lucier Oregon's only four-diamond restaurant rating from AAA for 2009.

*A: Exterior   **B:** Bar   **C:** Dining room*
***Photography:** William Vasquez*

A

B

Located on the third floor of the Luxor Hotel and Casino, in Las Vegas, Tacos and Tequilas is a Mexican cantina whose all-but-impossible-to-ignore design and award-winning lighting solve a novel problem. The 120-seat, 5,000-square-foot restaurant is part of the Luxor's signature atrium space, so it lacks ceilings or walls. Instead, the design team of Alvarez + Brock with Ann Kale Associates as lighting designer has created a glowing, abstract version of a sombrero that hovers overhead to establish a sense of place. Their 180-foot-long by 12-foot-wide assemblage of folded aluminum panels is pieced in a pattern featuring a dancing skeleton figure and internally illuminated with two rows of white LED light strips, making it easily visible from the casino floor below. It shares pride of place with a 25-foot by 65-foot photographic mural of a female matador that is as commanding as the sombrero, thanks to simple incandescent sign lighters. Lighting is also critical in defining El Salon, the restaurant's adults-only dining room, where pools of dimmed halogen lighting and two more highlighted photo murals of the female matador sustain a mood of intimate privacy. As a result, owner Michael Frey can rightfully declare, "This is not your grandma's cantina."

A: Entrance B and C: Dining area
Photography: William Vasquez

C

The Surrey Hotel, in Manhattan's Upper East Side, is both a familiar destination and a delightful discovery. Built in 1926 as a prestigious residential hotel, the Surrey has sheltered such celebrity residents as John F. Kennedy, Bette Davis and Claudette Colbert. Today, the Surrey has been reborn as a 222-room luxury boutique hotel, with interior design by Rottet Studio and lighting design by Ann Kale Associates. The renovation has transformed everything, from the entry, registration, lobby and Bar Pleaides (from renowned French chef Daniel Boulud), to conference rooms, spa, guestrooms, and suites,

following Rottet's concept of a New York City townhouse passed down through the generations. Interiors are sophisticated and sumptuous, employing a Coco Chanel-inspired color palette of black, white and pearl gray, and elegant transitional furnishings with a dash of modernism. The award-winning lighting accentuates each of the hotel's environments. So while the reception area features a laylight internally illuminated with indirect white LEDs, Bar Pleaides employs incandescents in Art Deco frosted glass sconces, incandescent pendants, halogen spotlights, and LEDs housed in coves and below the

seating. With such finely crafted interiors, the Surrey can keep creating memorable moments for generations of guests to come.

A: Reception B: Lobby C: Suite D: Bar Pleaides
Photography: *Tom McWilliam*

ANN KALE ASSOCIATES   Star Island Residence | Miami, Florida

A guardhouse stands at the entrance to Star Island, giving it the illusion of being a private community. But the man-made island in Biscayne Bay, within the City of Miami Beach, is a public neighborhood, albeit one for wealthy and famous individuals. It is here Ann Kale Associates served as lighting designer in creating an 8,000-square-foot residence for a music industry mogul. The architecture, interior design and lighting design are custom tailored to an owner who likes to cook while entertaining, fulfilling his request for a luxurious yet comfortable environment. Lighting plays a critical role in establishing the ambiance. To promote a seamless transition from indoor to outdoor within the mostly open floor plans, the lighting scheme features the same lighting in both zones. This technique causes the glass walls separating reflecting pools along the inside and outside of the perimeter to all but disappear, and gives the indoor thatched ceiling coffer an unmistakably outdoor feel. Elsewhere, warm lighting invites guests to the kitchen to watch and assist with preparations, and adds a festive touch to the large dinner parties in the dining room. In effect the lighting is inseparable from the overall environment in this exceptional space.

A: Exterior with swimming pool   B: Kitchen
C: Living room   D: Staircase/entry
***Photography:** Kim Sargent*

ANN KALE ASSOCIATES The City University of New York | Bernard and Anne Spitzer School of Architecture | New York, New York

It seems fitting that the Bernard and Anne Spitzer School of Architecture at the City University of New York emphasizes urban culture as a generator of ideas for programs and forms in the built environment. Appropriately, the city's only public school of architecture has moved into the new, 125,000-square-foot facility that has emerged from the gut renovation of an old school library, designed by Rafael Viñoly Architects with lighting design by Ann Kale Associates. RVAPC's architecture transforms the existing structure by cutting an atrium into the center to serve as a dynamic gallery for student work, and spans the atrium with crisscrossing bridges to promote circulation and provide exciting opportunities for study and socialization. The lighting figures prominently in the striking yet cost-effective project. Shallow fluorescent fixtures, custom designed by Ann Kale Associates, are surface mounted in all classrooms and the atrium while fluorescent wallwashers line corridor walls and metal halide uplights attach to columns to illuminate a Spartan, modern setting of white walls, gray concrete floors and brightly colored accent walls, providing a sense of order, purpose and excitement. With the nearly 40-year-old Spitzer School poised to move in new and interesting directions, its new home looks fit and ready.

A: Atrium roof **B:** *Circulation in the atrium*
C: Rooftop
Photography: *Bruce Demonte*

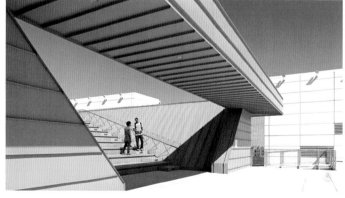

ANN KALE ASSOCIATES   Olio | MGM Grand | Las Vegas, Nevada

Great expectations are *de rigeur* in Las Vegas, so when New York restaurateur John Tunney III declared Olio, his new, 5,000-square-foot (front of house) Neo-Italian restaurant at MGM Grand, would be "worthy of the entertainment capital of the world," he clearly meant its décor along with its food and service. Designed by Jeffrey Beers International with Ann Kale Associates as lighting designer, Olio delivers an exciting experience that begins with the bar, leads to several dining areas, and concludes in the gelato bar. Contemporary interiors of wood, stone, leather and textiles smartly complement executive chef Clay Conley's lively menu, and the lighting—featuring fixtures custom designed by Ann Kale Associates—emphasizes their differences. For example, lighting creates a dark, seductive aura for the bar, directing guests to onyx tables lit by inground halogen uplights and custom pendants. Further on, the Pasta Bar shines with custom pendants over common tables, the lower dining area brightens its sweeping, red resin ceiling with custom pendants, and the upper dining area dramatizes its soaring white ceiling with color-changing, wall-mounted LED bubbles and a custom pendant designed by Jeffrey Beers International. For desert, the gelato bar displays its 40 flavors like jewels under sparkling spotlights.

A: Upper dining area   B: Bar   C: Gelato bar
D: Lower dining area
Photography: *Chris Wessling*

ANN KALE ASSOCIATES   Bouchon | Beverly Hills, California

Renowned chef Thomas Keller's fondness for his Bouchon restaurants, in Yountville, California, Las Vegas and now Beverly Hills, is evident in his comments on their French bistro cuisine. "These are foods that represent the most important kind of cooking there is because they're rooted in tradition," he observes. "So when I thought of opening a restaurant that's more casual than The French Laundry (another Ann Kale Associates project), I decided to explore and deepen the culinary heritage that I admire so much." To give Keller an 11,000- square-foot space "where people come to relax, talk and eat," interior designer Adam Tihany and lighting designer Ann Kale Associates created a romantic, comfortable and unmistakably Gallic Bouchon in Beverly Hills, comprising the reception and Bar Bouchon on the ground floor and the restaurant, bar, Champagne lounge and terrace dining upstairs. The lighting is especially impressive here. Besides enhancing the interior design, it meets LEED's strict

power allowance, using 2700K compact fluorescent lamps with color correction gels for custom decorative fixtures, and halogen and LED for all others. Even so, the state-of-the-art lighting technology does nothing to disturb the dreamy,

ochre-colored interiors of wood, ceramic tile, brass and mirrors, producing the perfect milieu for dishes such as roast chicken grand-mère.

A: *Dining room*   **B:** *Bar*
Photography: *Arthur Gray*

Aria Group Architects, Inc.

830 North Boulevard • Oak Park, IL 60301 • 708.445.8400 • 708.445.1788 (Fax)

www.ariainc.com

ARIA GROUP ARCHITECTS, INC.   LA Food Show | Beverly Hills, California

Success in restaurants often fuels more success, as Rick Rosenfield and Larry Flax, co-CEOs of California Pizza Kitchen, know well. However, to roll out the second restaurant for LA Food Show, their upscale and chic new chain, Rosenfield and Flax started from scratch in Beverly Hills. Seeking a fresh look for their dining concept, they asked Aria Group Architects to turn an early 20th-century industrial building into a sleek, 200-seat, 7,296-square-foot restaurant. The design team shrewdly let site conditions shape the environment. For example, to meet city requirements and showcase the interior to the street, the small storefront incorporated large areas of butt glazing. Existing bowstring trusses,

wood beams and brick walls expressed great character, so they were integrated into the contemporary interior of wood, stone and terrazzo. Although the owners didn't originally request a mezzanine, they accepted one to increase seating capacity—along with a striking, monumental stair to dramatize it. To improve depth of vision in the long, narrow space, the exhibition kitchen and bar line the long walls. The resulting space is warm, stylish and exciting, drawing the families, couples and businessmen LA Food Show has targeted for popular entrées like miso black cod and homemade meatloaf.

A: Main dining seating   ***B:*** *Bar*   ***C:*** *Storefront*
D: Main level, mezzanine and stair
Photography: *Anthony Gomez*

ARIA GROUP ARCHITECTS, INC.   P.F. Chang's | Corpus Christi, Texas

Attentive staff serving Chinese cuisine, wine and tempting desserts in a stylish, high-energy bistro environment has been a winning recipe for P.F. Chang's, a restaurant chain founded in 1993. Indeed, its new, 252-seat, 7,904-square-foot restaurant in Corpus Christi, Texas, designed by Aria Group Architects in close collaboration with Shawmut Design & Construction, displays all the characteristics that make the chain a nationwide success. But the Corpus Christi store's resemblance to other P.F. Chang's masks an increased commitment to sustainable design worthy of LEED Gold certification. Focusing on energy efficiency, the design incorporates innovative elements that stay within 10 percent of the typical construction budget and are available for future stores. Among numerous green features spread across the kitchen, main dining, bar dining and indoor/outdoor patio are Energy Star-rated equipment, low-flow plumbing fixtures, low-e glass, lighting featuring LED and CFL lamps, finishes and materials with recycled content, low-emitting carpet tile and composite wood, and a comprehensive energy monitoring system. None of this intrudes on the guest experience, which is framed by P.F. Chang's signature blend of classic Chinese style, contemporary design, and a palette of earthy red and orange tones. However, the establishment now knows sustainability goes very well with profitability.

A: Exterior B: Main dining   C: Bar dining
D: Corridor
Photography: *Larry Falke*

ARIA GROUP ARCHITECTS, INC.   Viper Alley | Lincolnshire, Illinois

Youthful residents of suburban Chicago's North Shore are thrilled to have a nightlife, thanks to Viper Alley, a new, "revolutionary, immersive music experience and entertainment venue" at the CityPark retail center in Lincolnshire. Designed by Aria Group Architects, the 18,400-square-foot facility constitutes a lively assemblage of activities under one roof. The "factory plush" space actually houses three separate venues linked by strategically placed portals: Viper Alley Live, a boutique concert venue, Viper Alley Lounge, a high-energy nightclub, and Viper Alley

Private Events, a flexible space for social and corporate gatherings. These venues form the heart of a larger, industrial-style environment—comprising a ticket office, reception desk, service bar, main bar, open pizza/sandwich oven cooking station, café, dining room, private dining room, banquet area, performance area with 12-foot by 27-foot stage and dance floor, built-in VIP lounge seating, VIP/Green Room, video, sound and lighting control booth, six bowling lanes, bowling lounge, restrooms and storage. What allows the diamond-in-the-rough design to work so smoothly,

judging from its enthusiastic crowds, are its scalable spaces, reconfigurable seating arrangements and versatile multi-media technology. From pre-show to late night, the transitions look seamless to patrons, letting the show go on and on.

A: Main bar   B: Ticket office and grand stair
C: Performance area   D: Open pizza/sandwich oven cooking station
Photography: *© Douglas A. Salin*

ARIA GROUP ARCHITECTS, INC. Nando's Peri-Peri | Silver Spring, Maryland

With chicken providing the foundation for so many food service businesses, diners may be surprised to find that there is always room for one more, including the new Nando's Peri-Peri in Silver Spring, Maryland, a 149-seat, 4,558-square-foot restaurant designed by Aria Group Architects. Nando's Peri-Peri is a global restaurant chain founded in South Africa in

1987 that serves Portuguese flame-grilled peri-peri chicken (peri-peri is the Portuguese pronunciation of pili-pili, the African birds-eye chili pepper) in 34 countries on five continents. Its third store in metropolitan Washington, D.C. maintains the fun, eclectic design identity of the chain by mixing authentic Portuguese/African art, artifacts and distressed finishes, reflecting the chicken recipe's Portuguese colonial African heritage, with contemporary architectural design elements. Thus, antique clay pots, twisted vines and South African artwork take their places among leather and fabric upholstered booths, brightly furnished with modern wood tables and flaming red chairs, that are grouped in three sections under a dark ceiling where circular soffits hover like orbiting planetary rings. An "aged" storefront completes the image by pairing existing

masonry with African iroko wood left unsealed to weather faster, hinting at the centuries-old roots of this new chicken on the block.

A: Rear of dining room   B: View of dining room towards storefront   C: Storefront D: Entrance
Photography: Anthony Gomez

ARNOLD SYROP ARCHITECTS

290 Fifth Avenue • New York, NY 10001 • 212.947.7070 • 212.643.8449 (Fax)

www.arnoldsyrop.com

ARNOLD SYROP ARCHITECTS   The Grove | Cedar Grove, New Jersey

Do pomp and circumstance belong in modern American life? Public enthusiasm for events such as the royal wedding of England's Prince William and Kate Middleton in April 2011 reminds us why communities welcome facilities like The Grove, an outstanding, two-story, 50,000-square-foot catering hall in Cedar Grove, New Jersey, designed by Arnold Syrop Architects to accommodate up to 725 guests. Within a modern building graced by Neoclassical architectural elements, the design can accommodate two or more major events simultaneously with style and efficiency, thanks to a floorplan that effectively organizes a Central Lobby, two ballrooms (a 4,500-square-foot Regency and a 10,616-square-foot Grand, which can be divided into two spaces), gallery, public bathrooms and kitchen on the main level, a gallery, function room, two bridal suites and public bathrooms on the mezzanine level, and a valet parking car pick-up lobby, function room, bathrooms, storage and staff functions on the lower level. The Grove's swift acceptance by the public appears to stem from form and function as well as careful attention to the sensibilities of the young people who represent one of its primary markets. Determined to differentiate The Grove from competitors, the owner, Second Gen Corporation, worked closely with Arnold Syrop Architects to develop a fresh, contemporary vision of important social and business events, balancing state-of-the-art technology and spatial concepts with aesthetic traditions that society continues to cherish. The result is a unique, modern environment that respects the past without surrendering to it. Of course, the

long, rectangular building also responds directly to on-site conditions at the attenuated, four-acre tract bordering Pompton Avenue, a major thoroughfare. Its geometry has dictated a central lobby and public bathrooms with a ballroom at each end, a configuration that lends itself to staging simultaneous events. Guests easily find their orientation via the Central Lobby, a two-story volume with domed ceiling and lounge, expressed on the exterior by the cylindrical bay adjacent to the porte cochère, that is dominated by the grand stairway connecting the main and mezzanine levels. In addition, individual spaces

A: Central lobby lounge   B: Exterior
C: Grand stairway in Central Lobby
***Overleaf:** Central Lobby*
***Photography:** Abbey Photography,*
Nicole Reiter,

ARNOLD SYROP ARCHITECTS

project their own distinctive identities through a color palette of neutral tones accented by strong punches of color, architectural detailing that features such contemporary touches as acrylic capitals on ballroom pilasters housing programmable LED lights linked to LEDs in the chandeliers, and a lighting scheme that combines chandeliers and other decorative fixtures with integrated and concealed architectural lighting, such as the petal-shaped sconces doubling as pilasters in the mezzanine gallery. Because even the smallest details count in events such as weddings and anniversaries, each bridal suite has a flat screen that lets the bridal party monitor the ballroom scene right up to the bride's formal entry.

A: Illuminated capital on ballroom pilaster
B: Bridal Suite C: Grand Ballroom with stairway to bridal suite D: Grand Ballroom

D

ARNOLD SYROP ARCHITECTS

A: Petal-shaped sconce in mezzanine gallery
B: Men's bathroom   C: Mezzanine gallery

AvroKO

224 Centre Street, Floor 3 • New York, NY 10013 • 212.343.7024

www.avroko.com

AvroKO   Social House | Crystal City Center | Las Vegas, Nevada

In a daring departure from the standard Las Vegas restaurant, AvroKO used a strong conceptual framework to shape its enclosed dining area and open dining terrace when designing Social House. Social House stands out because its contemporary interpretation of the microcosmic character of an old, walled Asian metropolis seems to throb with a genuine, self-sufficient life of its own. Like a city-within-a-city, the 280-seat, 10,000-square-foot restaurant connects its awkwardly long, winding space by organizing various bars and dining areas like urban neighborhoods along the length of the space. Thus, what resembles a traditional herbal pharmacy frames the entryway, featuring a giant stairwell filled with hundreds of glowing brass drawers. Other areas hint at communal markets with vintage scales, water buckets, fishing weights and a ceiling of large, internally lit birdcages, while the obligatory VIP room evokes a decadent opium den, covered in luxurious fabrics and illuminated by a chandelier of glass "opium pipes." Tempted by such distinctive interiors and an equally imaginative menu, crowds keep coming to explore Social House's miniature metropolis.

A: Reception lounge   B: Restroom   C: Sushi bar   D: Marketplace dining area   E: Newspaper lined dining area   F: Detail of newspaper reading room   G: Bar with birdcages and porcelain birds
***Photography:** Michael Weber*

D

E

F

AvroKO Bourbon Steak | Scottdale, Arizona

Since America's Southwest profoundly inspired such artists and architects as Georgia O'Keefe, Frank Lloyd Wright, Antoine Predock and Donald Judd, it was natural for AvroKO to design the new, 364-seat, 9,000-square-foot Bourbon Steak, in Scottsdale, Arizona, in response to the region's cultural tradition, unique environment and place in art history. But the design team wanted to make its own contribution to desert design—transcending any single period in time while incorporating such precedents as Arts & Crafts and Minimalism—to complement Bourbon Steak's forward-looking focus on all-natural, organic and hormone-free cuts of beef poached and finished over a wood-burning grill. To gather the separate genres, this modern American steakhouse exploits the tensions between opposing aesthetic values. For example, the positive and negative spaces within the building envelope at the Fairmont Scottsdale Princess, feature a dramatic void between a new, board-formed concrete wall plane and the face of the previous front of the building. Elsewhere, a wall of woven brass rods set against a mirror alludes to Minimalism's industrial precision while the reflection effectively doubles the space. As diners are quick to appreciate, Bourbon Steak brings fresh ideas to the visual arts as well as the culinary ones.

A: Entrance B: Cocktail lounge C: Banquette seating D: Dining room E: Entrance
F: Vaulted ceiling over dining room
Photography: *Michael Weber and Yuki Kuwana*

AvroKO Double Crown | New York, New York

What the 19th century British presence in Southeast Asia did to people and cultures is celebrated in the cuisine of Double Crown, a new, 150-seat restaurant on New York's revitalized Bowery, and its two-level, 3,600-square-foot interior. The pairing makes sense, given that Double Crown is the second restaurant designed, developed and owned by AvroKO and executive chef Brad Farmerie. Just as the menu explores how traditional British dishes were reborn through new tropical ingredients and sensibilities, the design reassembles British and Southeast Asian aesthetics in a modern way. Austere Western church architecture and iconography form an idiosyncratic union with Asian temples' colorful textures and patterns in the Main Dining Room, where British woodwork meets custom-designed caned furniture, teak coffered ceilings combine with industrial brass screens, antique Indian photographs glow in neon lighting, a quirky temple alter displays Eastern and Western artifacts, and salvaged steel lights merge with pulley-operated ceiling fans common throughout Southeast Asia. In the adjoining Panel Room, woodwork from a 19th-century apartment lines the walls, while the back lounge, Madam Geneva, contrasts delicate lace wall panels against metal screens and exposed brick. What better setting exists for Singapore laksa soup, miso-glazed bone marrow, or duck steamed buns?

A: Bar B: Main dining room C: Panel room
D: Restroom E: Corridor F: Madam Geneva
***Photography:** Michael Weber*

AvroKO Lily and Bloom | Hong Kong, China

Worlds old and new collide regularly in Hong Kong, a former British Crown Colony and modern business center serving the world's second largest economy. A fresh example is Lily and Bloom, a new 81-seat bar and 95-seat restaurant whose time traveling has fueled their instant popularity. When guests enter Lily, on the 6th floor of the sleek Hotel LFK, or Bloom, one floor below, two spaces totaling 9,000 square feet joined by an atrium staircase, they encounter the dense tapestry of patterns and finishes in fin de siècle New York and Paris café society. Lily is raw and lively in its seated bar backed by an ornate, cast-iron grill, chairs inspired by early 20th century transportation, private dining room and "The B!ind Pig" (a euphemism for a speakeasy), a cigar room incorporating salvaged wood and hardware. Bloom, quoting the grand hotel restaurants, brasseries and shopping arcades that flourished until Prohibition, offers a richly detailed, brasserie-style restaurant of tile, wood and wrought iron where guests can savor roasted salmon steak with caramelized fennel, foie gras in red wine reduction, and Iberico pork chops and spare ribs. As *Time Out Hong Kong* declared, "Quite simply, there is no other place like this in town."

A: Blind Pig, Lily ***B:*** *Main dining room, Bloom* ***C:*** *Balcony overlooking atrium, Lily* ***D:*** *Seated bar, Lily*
Photography: *Jason Lang*

BASKERVILL

101 S. 15th Street Suite 200 • Richmond, VA 23219 • 804.343.1010 • 804.343.0909 (Fax)

www.baskervill.com

BASKERVILL   Doubletree Palm Beach Gardens and Executive Meeting Center | Palm Beach Gardens, Florida

Business and leisure travelers on Florida's South Atlantic Coast seeking a sophisticated but more casual and contemporary alternative to lodging in West Palm Beach need search no farther than the new Doubletree Hotel & Executive Meeting Center, in Palm Beach Gardens. The 279- room Doubletree offers a chic, Zen-like contemporary setting with the latest amenities and services, designed by Baskervill, minutes from beaches in Juno and Singer Island and downtown West Palm Beach. Its construction has won LEED Silver certification— one of the region's first hotels so designated— because it was developed in accordance to sustainable design principles, and features an Executive Meeting Center and 50 guestrooms that are 99 percent allergen-free. Of course, its green design features are just part of a total guest experience that celebrates the South Florida lifestyle. Guests need not concern themselves with sustainability to enjoy the lobby, restaurant, cocktail lounge, coffee bar, swimming pool and fitness center, conservatory and 16,000-square-foot Executive Meeting Center. However, the abundant natural lighting, attractive contemporary furnishings in tropical-inspired colors and finishes, environmentally sensible and recycled building materials, purified interior air, and thoughtfully arranged wayfinding make a stay at the Doubletree rewarding in more ways than one.

A: Fusion Lounge   B: Oz Restaurant
C: Conservatory   D: Meeting room
E: Pre-function area   F: Lobby
Photography: *Cris Molina/The Photographers Gallery*

D

E

F

BASKERVILL Richmond Marriot Hotel and T-Miller's Sports Bar & Grill | Richmond, Virginia

A: Pod check-in *B: Liberty Bar* *C: T-Miller's*
Sports Bar & Grill *D: Lobby* *E: Guest suite*
F: Concierge Lounge
Photography: *Eric Heimlich/Steve Hinds, Inc.*

One of downtown Richmond's most popular hotels, the 410-room Richmond Marriott has emerged from a major renovation, designed by Baskervill, looking more desirable than ever for lodging, conducting business and socializing. Fresh design concepts are visible everywhere, from porte cochere and lobby to restaurant, fitness center and guest suites, as new floor plans, upgraded finishes, stylish furnishings and custom lighting enliven the guest experience. For example, the dynamic new lobby encourages gathering and conversation, thanks to its floor-to-ceiling waterfall, built-in televisions, intimate groupings of contemporary lounge seating, sleek wood-planked floor and ceiling inserts, and pod check-in. Likewise, T-Miller's Sports Bar & Grill calls out to sports fans with new, rich woods, colorful mosaic tiles, stainless steel bar fronts, dramatic light fixtures, a floor plan that lets customers gather around monitors showing their favorite sports, and a new, year-round patio with outdoor fire pit. Yet there's more to the revitalized Richmond Marriott, including a breezily open day/night bar and lounge, luxurious concierge lounge for VIP guests, retrofitted fitness center with new windows bringing daylight and views, and five refurbished guest suites boasting higher level finishes, new wet bars and jacuzzi bathrooms. The capital of the Commonwealth of Virginia deserves nothing less.

BASKERVILL Renaissance Portsmouth Hotel & Waterfront Conference Center |
Portsmouth, Virginia

A

Offering sweeping views of the waterfront and shipyards of Portsmouth, Virginia, home of the Norfolk Naval Shipyard and historic Olde Towne Portsmouth, the 249-room Renaissance Portsmouth Hotel & Waterfront Conference Center has burnished its appeal to business and leisure travelers with a stylish renovation, designed by Baskervill. The remodeling of two lobbies, two ballrooms, 70-seat amphitheater, restaurant, 244 guestrooms and five suites introduces a playful yet sophisticated environment, built around nautical-inspired colors, patterns, forms and textures, that highlights

Portsmouth's heritage and Marriott's Renaissance brand. Particular attention is focused on public facilities to pamper guests and support special events. In the rotunda, stately furnishings, a gleaming chandelier with matching sconces, and drapery that emphasizes the room's 14-foot tall windows achieve a timeless elegance ideal for business and social gatherings. The fireplace lounge, by contrast, encourages guests to relax, catch up on news and weather on the 52-inch flat screen television, sip cocktails at custom-designed circular sofas, or stay in touch with family, friends and colleagues via

computer stations, while cocktail cubbies manage the transition from lounge to restaurant with flexible seating and oversized drum lampshades. Whatever guests' agendas, the Renaissance Portsmouth extends a gracious and timely welcome to Portsmouth.

*A: Rotunda **B:** Guestroom **C:** Guestroom desk and office chair **D:** Fireplace lounge **E:** Cocktail cubby **F:** Corridor* **Photography:** *Bradley Hart Photography*

BASKERVILL   Hyatt Dulles Hotel and Executive Meeting Center | Herndon, Virginia

Airport hotels are appreciated by travelers when they deliver comfort, convenience and a sense of place seldom found in transportation centers, so recent renovations at the 316-room Hyatt Dulles at Dulles International Airport, in Herndon, Virginia, designed by Baskervill, will surely win guests' gratitude. The project, which consisted of a new entry experience, partly remodeled lobby, public space makeover, four new suites and a new executive meeting center, manages to be crisp, streamlined and functional with warm, inviting touches and enough green design features for LEED

Silver certification. At the heart of this successful transformation is the design team's awareness that guests want the latest in services and amenities as well as state-of-the-art technologies to be delivered within an attractive, distinctive and personalized environment. Thus, while the IACC executive meeting center is fitted with leading-edge technologies and ergonomic furnishings to give guests an ideal venue for meetings and teamwork, the space also provides carpet in custom patterns designed by a leading interior designer Patricia Lopez, low environmental impact wallcoverings

made from fused wood and latex, cherry and zebra wood tones, and metal and marble accents, infusing the space with absorbing detail and a decidedly non-institutional image—at Dulles International Airport, no less.

A: Executive Meeting Center   B: Express-O's
C: Guest suite   D: Lobby
Photography: *Joel Lassiter/Lassiter Photography, Earl Zubkoff/Essential Eye Photographics, LLC*

BG Studio International Inc.

264 West 40th Street, Suite 703 • New York, NY 10018 • 212.242.8273 • 212.242.8274 (Fax)

www.bgstudio.com

BG STUDIO INTERNATIONAL INC. Celebrity Cruise Solstice | Ft. Lauderdale, Florida

The much-anticipated arrival of the 122,000-ton Celebrity Solstice and Solstice class of ships in 2008 enabled Celebrity Cruises to develop its innovative concept of a refined boutique hotel within a large premium cruise ship. As travel professionals noted, superb interior architecture contributed significantly to the ship's success. Following a study of what today's discerning traveler wants, Celebrity asked design firms to translate new "Celebrity Life" enrichment and entertainment programs into effective interiors, entrusting BG Studio International to design five restaurants and bars. BG Studio's

award-winning designs not only honored the conventions of cruise ship design and strict rules on materials set by the International Maritime Organization, they introduced branded spaces that put fresh, transitional styles, focused layouts, imaginative furnishings, rich color schemes, luxurious materials and dramatic lighting in the service of Celebrity's lifestyle initiative. Thus, the Ensemble Lounge's café-style, 78-seat, 3,672-square-foot gathering place for pre-dinner and late night drinks, Murano's opulent, 76-seat, 2,160-square foot European setting for Continental cuisine, Michael's

Club's 52-seat, 1,598-square-foot university club-like refuge, Passport Lobby's sprawling, 117-seat, 5,940-square-foot yacht-inspired people-watching space, and Cellar Masters' 59-seat, 2,246-square-foot wine-tasting bar, rustic and cozy, give savvy, affluent guests dining-out choices they would expect on land.

A: Passport Bar B: Ensemble Lounge
C: Cellra Masters D: Michael's Club
E: Passport Lobby F: Murano
***Photography:** Craig Denis, used with permission of Royal Carribean Cruises Ltd.*

A

B

C

D

E

F

BG STUDIO INTERNATIONAL INC. 2010 Showtime Show House | The Big C Rooms | New York, New York

Cancer is a weighty subject treated in a light-hearted way in Showtime Networks' popular new comedy series, "The Big C," in which Cathy Jamison, a suburban wife and mother played by actress Laura Linney, changes her life after a terminal cancer diagnosis. Problematic as this story first seemed as entertainment, it became one of the most memorable themes for Showtime's third annual Showtime House, a showhouse in the Casa Hotel and Residences in midtown Manhattan celebrating the fall 2010 launch of Showtime's 2010-2011 scripted dramas. BG Studio International transformed a hallway, home office/closet, bathroom and bedroom into an environment portraying The Big C. The 500-square-foot space, themed according to the stages by which the mind processes shocking news such as a cancer diagnosis and developed through a joyous, life-affirming use of color, form, furnishings and lighting, drew favorable media attention. Guests entered the Hall of Cognition, a hallway lined with stills from the show, proceeded to the Contemplation Room, an hourglass-shaped space reiterating the show's strongest icon, and the Confusion Room, an altar-like niche, before reaching the Clarity Room, a calm and happy place complete with grass, rabbits, a sofa suspended like a swing and presumably a beatific Cathy.

A: Confusion Room   B: Rabbit in Clarity Room
C: Hall of Cognition   D: Contemplation Room
E: Clarity Room
Photography: *Andrew French, courtesy of Showtime Networks*

An unprecedented world awaits guests aboard Royal Caribbean's Oasis of the Seas and its sister ship, Allure of the Seas. The ships share the distinction of being the world's largest passenger vessels, each measuring 1,187 feet long, weighing 225,000 gross tons, and carrying some 5,600 people. Not surprisingly, their interior architecture stresses spaciousness and light, even in the areas lacking natural light that are inevitable within great volumes of space, so passengers always feel free and unconstrained. These qualities are abundantly present, along with distinctive aesthetics, clear spatial organization, and effective use of color, furnishings and lighting, in BG Studio International's designs for the ships, including a restaurant, 150 Central Park, and three bars and lounges, Comedy Live, Jazz on Four and Rising Tides. Since each facility confronts unique circumstances of location and purpose, its space is precisely tailored to its context. For example, 150 Central Park is a 77-seat, 2,160-square-foot restaurant that uses Versailles' "Le Petit Trianon" as its inspiration to produce an intimate, romantic milieu—an enchanted palace in a magical forest—featuring curving, wood-paneled walls, overscaled, throne-like chairs, floral-patterned textiles and carpet, and intricately detailed, custom-designed lighting. By contrast, Comedy Live derives its urban ambiance from the subways of New York (Oasis) and London (Allure), drawing guests through a tunnel-like portal into a 114-seat, 1,836-square-foot space arranged around a stage and outfitted with such reminders of life underground as exposed steel columns and beams, bright, primary colors, and seating and lighting that evoke subway stations and passenger cars. A different urban mood prevails in Jazz on 4, where the models are Prohibition-era Chicago (Oasis) and New Orleans' French Quarter (Allure), resulting in a 98-seat, 2,225-square-foot nightclub of rich textile and leather upholstery, velvet drapes, crystal table lamps and a backlit

A: Jazz on 4, stage B: Jazz on 4, lounge seating C: 150 Central Park, fabric panel D: Rising Tides
Photography: *Craig Denis, used with permission of Royal Caribbean Cruises Ltd.*

BG Studio International Inc.

stage, more noire for the former and more daring for the latter. But the most unusual space is surely Rising Tides (Allure only), a 32-seat, 518-square-foot bar on a moving platform shuttling between Deck 5 and Deck 8 while guests enjoy their beverages, inspired by the tides and the moon in its pearlescent leather-upholstered bar stools and tide-shaped communal bar table. Though each space stands alone in form and function, all add character and distinction to ships lauded by people and organizations ranging from Oprah Winfrey (Allure joined her list of Oprah's Favorite Things) to *Travel Weekly* (Oasis swept its awards as Best and Most Innovative Cruise Ship).

A: Comedy Live, entrance *B:* Comedy Live, stage

C² Limited Design Associates, LLC

Generations of families visiting Hershey, Pennsylvania, home of the Hershey Company since founder Milton Hershey built his chocolate factory there in 1905 and beloved tourist attraction ("The Sweetest Place on Earth"), have happily surrendered to the delectable comforts of the 278-room Hotel Hershey, a Mediterranean-style facility completed in 1933. Accordingly, the hotel's new, $67-million, LEED Silver-certified "Grand Expansion" respectfully upgrades the front entrance while adding ten Woodside Cottages for luxury guest lodging, a Meeting Cottage, swimming complex, ice-skating rink, new recreation area, 130-seat Harvest Restaurant, and seven new boutique shops. Award-winning interiors, designed by C² Limited Design Associates, simultaneously introduce world-class accommodations and preserve the traditional Amish-inspired ambiance. That's why the new, open lobby's classic architecture and stained glass ceiling project Old World grandeur, the charming Woodside Cottages gather spacious bedrooms around great rooms with stone fireplaces, the shops introduce an elegant retail corridor, and the Harvest Restaurant combines an 80-seat family-style dining room with other facilities in the manner of a country estate home. Ted J. Kleisner, president and CEO of Hershey Entertainment & Resorts Company, praises C² Limited, saying, "Their experience, background and industry knowledge made them the perfect choice for a project of this magnitude."

A: Guest bedroom, Woodside Cottages
B: Patio dining room, Harvest Restaurant
C: Reception lobby   D: Bar lounge, Harvest Restaurant   E: Great room, Woodside Cottages
F: Family-style dining room, Harvest Restaurant
Photography: *Tim Lee*

A

A new era has begun for the Greenbrier Resort, in White Sulphur Springs, West Virginia, the fabled host of VIPs since 1778, as the developer of the Greenbrier Sporting Club, a master planned, private, gated residential community of some 500 residences on the Resort's 6,500-acre estate. How skillfully the Club preserves the Resort's distinctive character in bringing five-star service to its incomparable setting can be seen at The Summit Lodge, one of various amenities at The Summit Village, a community of 56 home sites at the peak of Greenbrier Mountain. The interiors of the 7,500-square-foot Summit Lodge, designed by C[2] Limited Design Associates, offer such attractions as a 40-seat dining room, a signature bar and lounge, a covered porch, and a game room occupying a reconstructed 200-year-old log cabin, all within the context of rugged oak-and-cedar-frame construction evoking the great 19th-century Adirondack family compounds. C[2] Limited's approach to the design uses the simple elegance and informality of a country retreat as a foil for the Resort's magnificent landscape. Blending native, reclaimed timber and quarried stone with a lively mixture of formal and rustic traditional furnishings, the design has produced a classic lodge of effortless charm and comfort.

*A: Dining room **B:** Patio dining **C:** Bar and lounge **D:** Coatroom **E:** Game room* ***Photography:*** *Josh Gibbons*

C² LIMITED DESIGN ASSOCIATES   Turks & Caicos Sporting Club | Ambergris Cay
Turks & Caicos, British West Indies

Originally settled by the Taino Indians, colonized by England in the 17th century, and then abandoned to nature, Ambergris Cay is a 1,100-acre island in the Turks and Caicos, British West Indies that is now a private equity community offering luxury beachfront home sites. Turks & Caicos Sporting Club at Ambergris Cay represents a triumph of planning, logistics and determined effort, overcoming the initial lack of infrastructure, running water, electricity or island inhabitants. Prospective members can easily sample its lifestyle, thanks to the opening of Calico Jack Pavilion, a fine dining venue, and 12 villas built by an international developer, all featuring interiors designed by C² Limited Design Associates. Calico Jack combines indoor and outdoor dining in a beach setting of spectacular beauty. Its high-end appointments subtly acknowledge demanding environmental conditions, incorporating fabrics treated with sun and water repelling technology, durable mahogany furniture, metal galvanized to prevent rusting, and sophisticated lighting supplementing sunshine and starlight, while offering guests a gracious, British Colonial-style milieu. By contrast, the 12 residences combine the British Colonial feel with the lightness of Swedish painted furniture, custom lighting fixtures and colonial era-inspired accessories in a turnkey furnishings package to make luxurious barefoot living an everyday reality.

A: Outdoor dining, Calico Jack B: Bedroom, residence C: Living room, residence D: Living/dining suite, residence E: Bar, Calico Jack
Photography: *Steve Passmore/Provo Pictures*

C² LIMITED DESIGN ASSOCIATES   The Greenbrier | North Lobby, Theater Hall, Prime 44 West | White Sulphur Springs, West Virginia

Can history be improved? Consider the renovations designed by C² Limited Design Associates at the fabled Greenbrier Resort, the 682-room landmark established in 1778 in White Sulphur Springs, West Virginia. Inspired by signature interiors from the great Dorothy Draper, C² Limited worked with the Greenbrier's historian to reproduce archival photographs and documents for a glowing showcase of history in the Theater Hall, a 120-foot-long hallway leading to a 300-seat movie theater with newly refurbished doors. Not only do guests linger among its attractive displays, comfortable reading chairs and elegant writing desks, movie attendance has soared from one largely empty screening to two crowded screenings each evening. Similarly, the North Lobby has been brought to life with a Draper-inspired garden theme linking custom-designed seating, carpeting and chandeliers to existing Palladian windows. As for Prime 44 West, its emergence as a popular steakhouse in partnership with West Virginia native and NBA legend Jerry West (honoring West's number at the LA Lakers) started with a limited budget and tight deadline, salvaged the best of a previous restaurant, and added such essentials as West's sports memorabilia and design cues from Draper to evoke a traditional gentlemen's club that outscores its predecessors nightly 150 to 60.

A: Theater Hall B: North Lobby
C: Prime 44 West
Photography: *Robin Hood and Eric Adkins (North Lobby, Theater Hall), Tim Lee (Prime 44 West)*

CLEO DESIGN

CLEO DESIGN Seminole Hard Rock Hotel & Casino | High Limit Lounge and Private Dining Room | Hollywood, Florida

Players in the VIP High Limit Gaming Room at the Seminole Hard Rock Hotel & Casino, in Hollywood, Florida, can anticipate experiences that their fellow patrons will never know. One of their newest privileges is as delectable as it is exclusive: an invitation to the luxurious High Limit Lounge and Private Dining Room, a 1,168-square-foot, 46-seat facility, designed by Cleo Design. Here they will enjoy extraordinary food and beverage service provided by a professional staff using an exhibition kitchen equipped with the latest professional cooking equipment. To ensure that the décor is appropriate to the occasion, the design team has crafted a contemporary environment of rich leather and suede surfaces, stylish furniture, plush carpeting and gleaming hardwood floors, illuminated by sophisticated lighting that includes indirect wall art niches and decorative glass bubbles suspended from the ceiling as well as specific task lighting for the staff. A choice of traditional dining table, banquette and counter seating gives the dining room flexibility to host anything from an intimate gathering to a stage for a visiting celebrity chef. For high limit guests, the passage between the gaming tables and the dining tables now heralds yet another rewarding VIP experience.

A: Exhibition kitchen   B: Counter seating
C: Banquette seating   D: Entry
Photography: *Francis George*

D

CLEO DESIGN   Cirque du Soleil's Viva ELVIS | Aria Resort & Casino at City Center | Las Vegas, Nevada

The King of Rock 'n' Roll is back in the house at Cirque du Soleil's Viva ELVIS, a spectacular, 219,000-square-foot, 1,840-seat live performance venue that recently opened in the Aria Resort & Casino at City Center, Las Vegas. Designed by Cleo Design to house the fusion of dance, acrobatics and live music honoring Elvis Presley, the showroom comprises a theater, box office, food and beverage space, and pre-function area. Besides meeting the technical demands of live performances, the project skillfully creates a contemporary-style grand theater that conforms to the world class architecture of

City Center—MGM/Mirage's ambitious urban complex employing some of the world's leading architects—while projecting the warmth and intimacy of a classic "Vegas" showroom. Key to the innovative scheme is the way the opulent theater interior of rosewood and velour replicates the experience of a conventional lounge of upholstered booths through custom banquettes outfitted with individual flip-up seats. Not to be outdone, the lobby also offers an authentic "Vegas" experience of glitz and glamour, combining backlit acrylic wall panels, chrome and gem-like finishes, a deep black

galaxy granite floor and rosewood millwork. Even the theater door handles hint at the jewelry that was famously fit for the King.

A: Show logo   ***B:*** *Food and beverage area*
C: *Pre-function area and doors to theater*
Photography: *Studio West*

CLEO DESIGN   Indiana Live! Casino | Shelbyville, Indiana

To bring Las Vegas-style excitement to gaming venues in distant locations like Kansas City, Biloxi and Atlantic City, high-energy "Vegas" glitz is often successfully paired with a timeless design reflecting local culture. Such is the case with the new, 82,281-square-foot, 1,733-slot Indiana Live! Casino, in Shelbyville, Indiana. Its beckoning interiors, designed by Cleo Design, comprise the Casino, Casino Center Bar, Makers Mark Steakhouse, NASCAR Café, Poker Room, Mosaic Club/Lounge,

Gold Room High Limit Players Lounge, Platinum High Limit Players Lounge, High Limit Gaming Area and Lounge, and honor both "Vegas" glamour and Hoosier heritage. Within the Casino, for example, the bright carpet, coffered ceiling, golden-hued upholstery and copper chandeliers alter their appearance day and night, thanks to sophisticated lighting. Other spaces at Indiana Live! are similarly nuanced in form and function. So while the Poker Room sequesters players in a well-lit space with

A: Casino   B: Mosaic Club/Lounge   C: Poker Room   D: Gold Room High Limit Players Lounge
Photography: *Peter Malinowski*

D

CLEO DESIGN

neutral colors, ergonomic seating and a video screen array to support intense focus on the game, the High Limit Gaming Lounges give them an opulent environment for self-service buffet or full bar/lounge amenities, and the Makers Mark Steakhouse envelopes them in the warm and inviting amber glow of vintage and private stock whisky bottles that handsomely frame a dazzling exhibition kitchen.

A: *High Limit Gaming Lounge Restroom*
B: *Makers Mark Steakhouse*
Photography: *Peter Malinowski*

Cleo Design in Collaboration With Wynn Design & Development
Wynn Encore | Eastside Lounge | Las Vegas, Nevada

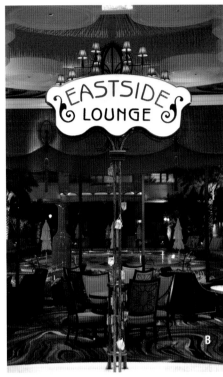

In a city where luxury is commonplace, casino developer Steve Wynn is celebrated for upping the ante, and his Encore at Wynn Las Vegas provides a good example. The 2,034-room Encore became the second tower on the grounds of the 2,716-room Wynn Las Vegas in 2008, three years after the resort opened with an on-site Ferrari-Maserati dealership. As always, Wynn redefined Las Vegas-style luxury with ever more lavish accommodations, finishes, amenities and entertainment options. His passion for making guests feel like royalty is evident in the Encore's new, 4,492-square-foot,

146-seat Eastside Lounge, designed by Cleo Design with Wynn Design & Development. The space was designed as a flexible indoor/outdoor environment where an early morning meeting ambiance yields to an afternoon cocktail setting overlooking the resort's pool, followed by an evening club featuring ceiling projection screens and a mobile DJ podium. In addition, the design had to visually relate to both the adjacent Casino as well as the pool. The design teams creative solution matches contemporary colors and traditional themed furnishings with a wool carpet's random, swirling pattern under soft

lights from dual bars buffering the Lounge from the Casino, adding hand-selected rock crystals as the kind of over-the-top embellishment Wynn's loyal fans expect.

A: Lounge seating   B: Entry   C: View from outdoor pool
Photography: *Studio West*

CLEO DESIGN   Seminole Hard Rock Hotel & Casino | Casino and VIP Areas Floor Addition | Tampa, Florida

Everybody loves a winner, and that's what the public calls the Seminole Hard Rock Hotel & Casino, in Tampa, Florida. Indeed, the Hard Rock has won enough business from players drawn to its 90,000-square-foot Casino, 12-story, 250-room Hotel, and vibrant mix of restaurants and bars, live entertainment, conference center, recreational facilities, spa and fitness center, and retail shopping that it has expanded to satisfy demand. The recently completed Casino and VIP Areas Floor Addition, designed by Cleo Design, is a new,

46,413-square-foot, 1,095-slot gaming floor that provides a Casino and Casino Bar, High Limit Lounge, second-level public area and monumental Grand Staircase to convey the public to it all. Because of the design's imaginative play on the Hard Rock style, the new gaming floor does more than complement the existing Casino, introducing a new and fresh experience for loyal customers and newcomers alike. The grand staircase, for example, cascades through a dynamic water feature that is animated by light from rock video images

projected through the water. From the Grand Staircase, the excitement builds, driven by a design blending the latest in technology with millwork cases that display music memorabilia, enticing customers to enjoy the new gaming floor.

*A: High Limit Lounge **B:** Casino **C:** Cashier
D: Corridor **E:** Grand Staircase and water feature*
Photography: *Francis George*

CLEO DESIGN   Rivers Casino | Pittsburgh, Pennsylvania

From its vantage point on Pittsburgh's North Shore next to Heinz Field, the new, 130,973-square-foot Rivers Casino features stunning views of the Ohio River and Pittsburgh skyline along with exciting attractions more commonly associated with Las Vegas, including nearly 3,000 slot machines, 86 table games, nine restaurants and bars, a 1,000-seat riverside amphitheater and live music. The community's swift acceptance of Rivers Casino is strongly supported by sleek, high-style interiors designed by Cleo Design, including the Casino,

Casino Bar and Casino Lounge, High Limit Gaming Area and High Limit Gaming Lounge, Deli, Drum Bar and Grand View Buffet, which beguile patrons by blending "Vegas" contemporary glitz with traditional upscale imagery. Consider Rivers' iconic, glass-enclosed Drum Bar. Exploiting a panoramic view of the river and downtown, the 80-foot-high space basks in sunlight by day and glows like a beacon by night, thanks to light displays from the spectacular, 60-foot-high light fixture above its 360-degree bar. Yet, just steps away, the High

Limit Gaming Lounge romances patrons with the warmth and intimacy of a traditional country club, featuring wood paneling, wood-beamed ceiling, two-sided fireplace and dark, wood-framed furniture set against a gold and brown color scheme. Who says opposites don't attract?

A: Casino   B: Cashier   C: 360-degree bar at Drum Bar   D: Entry to Casino   E: Drum bar at night
Photography: *Brad Feinknopf*

E

CLEO DESIGN   Blue Chip Casino Resort & Spa | Michigan City, Indiana

A compelling reason people visit casinos and resorts is to escape their daily routines, and the new Blue Chip Casino Resort & Spa, in Michigan City, Indiana, provides a seductive destination. Among its numerous distinctions is an unusual building shape that offers panoramic views of the Great Lakes but imposes curving forms on its interiors. Convinced that working with the curves was more fruitful than fighting them, Cleo Design designed the registration, convention promenade, meeting rooms, 18,000-square-foot ballroom, 300-room hotel tower and 12,900-square-foot spa to exploit curvilinear space. Instead of recessing the doorways to guest rooms from the corridor, Cleo Design purposefully located the doors on the edge of the curved walls to enhance the effect of a visual wave. A similar approach was taken to the ceiling

A: Registration desk   B: Spa reception
C: Salon   D: Meeting room pre-funtion area
Photography: *Bukva Imaging Group*

CLEO DESIGN

of the corridor, where the design team produced a surface that ebbs, flows and meanders. The latest comforts and conveniences were not ignored either. Thus, guest suites all boast state-of-the-art room control systems located both at room entries and bed headboards, and the spa features separate men's and women's lounges that can merge into one large room for special events like a "girls' night out." There's no reason to stay home now.

A: Suite bedroom   *B: Suite bathroom*
C: Guest bathroom   *D: Guest bedroom*

DESIGN GROUP CARL ROSS INC

115 Main Street • El Segundo, CA 90245 • 310.333.1982 • 310.333.1978 (Fax)

www.designgroupcarlross.com

DESIGN GROUP CARL ROSS INC   Hilton Grand Waikikian | Honolulu, Hawaii

Families staying at the Grand Waikikian, a new, upscale timeshare occupying a 38-story, 355-room tower on the grounds of the Hilton Hawaiian Village in Honolulu's fabled Waikiki oceanfront district, enjoy the best of two worlds—the charm of an old Hawaiian grand hotel combined with the comfort of a modern residence. In an award-winning interior design by Design Group Carl Ross encompassing the lobby and all public areas, standard villa units, penthouse units, Penthouse Lounge, and Arrival and Departure Lounge, the Grand Waikikian provides a luxurious, expansive and highly livable environment where Hawaiian style, indigenous reproductions and commissioned local art effortlessly commingle. What makes the setting so distinctive is the equal attention paid to both grand spaces and intricate details. The property's highly symmetrical, multi-level and multi-layer architectural interiors are enriched by warm and inviting finishes and furnishings that include mahogany veneer wainscot and pilasters, stained mahogany ceilings, porcelain ceramic floor tile, custom imported wool axminster carpeting, monolithic tropical wood carvings, and custom-designed table and floor lamps and chandeliers. The Grand Waikikian earned the American Resort Development Association's prestigious Project of Excellence award.

A: Lobby and registration   B: Suite bathroom C: Suite bedroom   D: Concierge and Reflecting Pool
Photography: *David Phelps*

A

Offering an elegant, comfortable and exclusive refuge for social and recreational activities, The Club at Flying Horse flourishes as the centerpiece of Flying Horse, a new luxury planned community in Colorado Springs, Colorado developed by the Classic Companies. The members-only club, which comprises a 48,000- square-foot Athletic Club and Spa, 40,000-square-foot Golf Clubhouse, and private, 18-hole Tom Weiskopf Signature Golf Course, is distinguished by award-winning interiors, designed by Design Group Carl Ross, that simultaneously focus attention on spectacular mountain views and provide unique spaces inspired by Tuscan and Colorado Mountain design themes. As a result, the extensive facilities, including a lobby, cardio areas, spa with four treatment rooms, men's and women's locker rooms, steam, sauna, beverage bar, pro shop, restaurant and pool deck in the Athletic Club, and a lobby, pro shop, men's and women's locker rooms, ballroom, boardrooms and three restaurants in the Golf Clubhouse, convey a genuine sense of place. Timeless building materials such as Venetian plaster, fieldstone, wood trim, wood beam ceilings, and wool axminster carpet

combine with eclectic, casually elegant furnishings, custom chandeliers and commissioned art to establish an inviting, residential feel that perfectly complements the majestic landscape outside.

A: Restaurant B: Corridor and boardroom
C: Spa relaxation area D: Fireplace lounge in lobby
Photography: *Robert Miller*

D

DESIGN GROUP CARL ROSS INC   Hyatt Siesta Key Beach | Sarasota, Florida

Owners at Hyatt Siesta Key Beach appreciate that the fractional resort represents more than its luxurious, fully furnished, 1,865- to 2,920- square-foot family vacation homes, its spectacular, 300-foot private beach of quartz-white sand, or its full-service Cabana Club, offering a swimming pool, poolside cabanas, café and more, minutes from Siesta Key and Sarasota on Florida's Gulf Coast. Indeed, the interior design by Design Group Carl Ross introduces luxury with an environmental conscience. Sustainable features range from synthetic stone used in countertops to offset demand for natural stone, Energy Star appliances and low-flow plumbing fixtures to a footbridge spanning over the delicate dune area and low nighttime lighting protecting indigenous sea turtles. Of course, green design also embellishes the interiors, which encompass 44 residences grouped around central, double-loaded corridors, fitness center and spa, men's and women's locker rooms, sauna and steam rooms, business center, pool area, registration lobby and member's lounge. Sumptuous living rooms, for example, feature hand-woven Thai rugs, custom media cabinets housing Bose surround-sound systems, 50-inch flat-screen TVs, custom-designed lighting fixtures and generous sofas upholstered with rich Italian fabrics, demonstrating how state-of-the-art services and technologies can seamlessly support casual yet opulent contemporary beach living.

A: Living room as seen from dining room
B: Master Bedroom   C: Master Bathroom
D: Swimming pool with poolside cabanas
Photography: *Robert Miller*

A

In anticipation of its repositioning from a flagged Hollywood hotel to the new 160-room Hollywood Heights Hotel, the owners of this independent and decidedly relaxed boutique hotel wanted to take advantage of its premium location just blocks from the Hollywood Bowl. Design Group Carl Ross was commissioned to design the restaurant and bar to complement the hotel and, more importantly, to attract patrons on its own. The 3,000-square-foot, 116-seat Hideout Restaurant meets the need artfully with a covered entry terrace lounge whose unmistakable street appeal draws guests to the sexy, colorful and unabashedly hip bar and restaurant. To build the layered look of openness and intimacy that makes the terrace lounge so compelling, the design team created a dynamic composition using such elements as a candle fireplace, millwork screens, wood plank flooring, bamboo, suspended glass spheres, and a ceiling that selectively reveals slivers and coves of light. Contemporary lounge furnishings that are as comfortable as they are stylish complete the picture, making The Hideout an enjoyable restaurant and casual bar by day and a more sophisticated ultra-lounge by night. The result is so appealing that the restaurant and bar speaks to business people and hipsters alike.

A: Terrace lounge **B:** *Booth seating*
Photography: *Design Group Carl Ross inc*

HART HOWERTON

10 East 40th Street • New York, NY 10016 • 212 683 5631 • 212 481 3768 (Fax) • ny@harthowerton.com

One Union Street • San Francisco, CA 94111 • 415 439 2200 • 415 439 2201 (Fax) • sf@harthowerton.com

57 Great Suffolk Street • London, United Kingdom SE1 0BB • +44 (0) 20 7593 3320 • +44 (0) 20 7620 0971 (Fax) • uk@harthowerton.com

1610 West Tower, Shanghai Centre, 1376 Nanjing Road West • Shanghai, China 200040 • +1 86 21 6279 8364 • +1 86 21 6279 8610 (Fax) • china@harthowerton.com

www.HartHowerton.com

Hart Howerton   Kuki'o | Kona Coast, Hawaii

Modeled after an historic Hawaiian fishing village, Kuki'o is a 660-acre private beach club and golf community—the only one of its kind on the Big Island of Hawaii—in Kailua-Kona, designed by Hart Howerton as master planner, architect and landscape architect for a development group comprising Discovery Land, Rockpoint Group, the Getty Trust and Hawaii Land Company. The project's goal has been to create an environment based on Hawaii's history culture, traditions and natural setting. Accordingly, Kuki'o's buildings and landscape environment seamlessly combine traditional Hawaiian construction materials and methods with state-of-the-art building technologies and principles of sustainable design. The impressive outcome includes the 34,000 square-foot Beach Club, with pavilions for the lodge, dining facilities and spa at the heart of the community; the 18-hole championship golf course and 10-hole short course, both designed by Tom Fazio; the 110 cottages and 150 home sites of varying sizes and configurations; and the distinctive

grounds of preserved major lava flows, beach and tropical landscape, presenting the best of Hawaiian life—indoor and outdoor.

A: Spa pavillion and pool   B: Mauka Lands Golf Clubhouse   C: Spa vanity   D: Dining pavilion   E: Outdoor bath   F: Beach Club
Photography: *Discovery Land Co., Mary E. Nichols*

F

HART HOWERTON   El Dorado Golf & Beach Club | Cabo San Lucas, Mexico

Golfers and their families were delighted when Discovery Land Company unveiled El Dorado Golf & Beach Club in Cabo San Lucas, Mexico, a luxury beach and golf community boasting one mile along the Baja Peninsula—and a spectacular championship Jack Nicklaus Signature golf course. Working closely with the client, the project team, including Hart Howerton, architect, GV Arquitectos, associate architect, egroup, landscape architect and pool designer, and Brayton & Hughes Design Studio, interior designer, transformed the steeply sloping, 520-acre site into a family-oriented community and club with 120 villas and 84 custom home sites. Hart Howerton decisively shaped El Dorado by designing the Beach & Golf Club House, Mercado/Sales Center, Dining, Spa, Gatehouse, Pro Shop, Beach Bar, Children's Center, Cardio Pavilion and

Spinning/Movement Center, encompassing 63,224 square feet overall. The firm is especially proud of the innovative service tunnel that feeds front- and back-of-house operations, keeping the latter invisible to members, and the Beach & Golf Club House, whose spa, fitness center, members' boutique shops, men's and women's lounge and locker areas, swimming facilities, indoor/outdoor dining areas, and children's activity center consistently draw compliments for their excellence, including this comment from the client: "This is the finest clubhouse in our portfolio."

A: Gatehouse B: Club House C: Beach Bar
D: Outdoor dining at Club House E: Infinity pool
Photography: *Discovery Land Co., Francisco Estrada, John Sutton*

HART HOWERTON Palmetto Bluff | Bluffon, South Carolina

Known as one of the wildest and most beautiful places in the Carolina Lowcountry, Palmetto Bluff is an 18,000-acre barrier island in Bluffton, South Carolina that is being developed as an exclusive resort community based on sustainable design the majestic landscape, and the indigenous qualities of the early coastal villages in the region. A key component of the project is Wilson Village, where Hart Howerton has served as architect, planner and landscape architect on a development team with Crescent Resources as owner/developer, and Auberge Resorts as hotel operator for the Inn at Palmetto Bluff, DWG, Inc. as MEP engineers, David C. Sladek, PE as structural engineer, Charles M. Salter Associates, Inc. as acoustical engineer, Thomas & Hutton Engineering as civil engineer, Craig Roberts Associates as lighting designer, Cini-Little as kitchen designer, and Fraser Construction, Inc. as general contractor.

Fashioned after an historic coastal town, the pedestrian-oriented Village forms the heart of a settlement within a maritime forest and land preserve that is now protected in perpetuity as open space. The Village includes such major buildings as The Inn at Palmetto Bluff, a luxury Auberge Resorts hotel comprising the River House (29,000 square feet),

A: River House Inn at Palmetto Bluff
B: Cottage   *C: Suite interior*   *D: Porch of cottage at the Inn*   *E: Outdoor dining at the Inn*
Photography: *Josh Savage Gibson, Wilson Associates, Auberge Resorts, Eric Embry, Eric Prine*

50 Cottages (115,000 square feet) and Spa (10,000 square feet), the May River Golf Clubhouse, the 11,000 square-foot gathering place and support facility for Palmetto Bluff's Jack Nicklaus Signature Golf Course, the Canoe Club (9,600 square feet), Fitness Center, Recreation Center and Pool Complex, plus numerous other structures. In addition, Hart Howerton has also been retained to provide master planning and design guidelines for the Village's Town Square and 2,900 home sites on 13,000 acres, with configurations ranging from Village homes to waterfront and golf course homes and even "Family Compounds" as large as 25 acres. As guests of the award-winning Inn at Palmetto Bluff already know, the resort is well on its way to establishing itself as an enchanted place to play and live just minutes from Savannah and Hilton Head Island.

A: The Canoe Club   B: Restaurant and bar at the Canoe Club

Haverson Architecture

63 Church Street • Greenwich, CT 06830 • 203.629.8300 • 203.629.8399 (Fax)

www.haversonarchitecture.com

Haverson Architecture Gabriele's Italian Steakhouse | Greenwich, Connecticut

Suppose you're a seasoned restaurateur like Danny Gabriele, whose family has served the public for years at 35 Church Street in Greenwich, Connecticut, looking for a fresh business opportunity with Jody Pennette, president of cb5 Restaurant Group, a noted restaurant consultant and operator. You realize that Greenwich, one of Fairfield County's legendary old, moneyed communities, needs an Italian steakhouse. Since Greenwich abounds in fine dining venues, you make sure everything is right from day one at Gabriele's Italian Steakhouse,

including the 50-table, 160-seat, 7,500-square-foot space, designed by Haverson Architecture. That's why the open, informal and country club-like interior has significantly reworked the existing space. Shifting structural columns to open up spaces, the new environment—comprising a bar, lounge, main and small dining areas, wine room/private dining, kitchen and restrooms—lets patrons feel intimately secluded yet part of a larger scene. Seated at tables, booths, banquettes or the bar, everyone can enjoy privacy while noting who's coming and going. Appointed in

dark wood floors and trim, Venetian plaster walls, coffered ceilings and fireplaces, Gabriele's also provides an irresistible venue for towers of seafood, parchment-thin ravioli, hearty salads, flavorful chicken and, of course, thick, juicy, perfectly seared steak. Buon appetito!

*A: Wine room** **B: Bar** **C: Main dining area**
D: Small dining area
Photography: *Peter Paige*

B

C

D

Restaurateurs know when a space feels right, so when Boston-based Kenneth Himmel teamed with London-based Marlon Abela to open Bistro du Midi, a new, 175-seat, two-story, 5,000-square-foot Provencal restaurant across the street from Boston's Public Garden, designed by Haverson Architecture, everyone realized the existing premises needed reworking. Himmel and Abela wanted an informal downstairs bistro, complete with a horseshoe-shaped bar and outdoor café, and a formal upstairs dining room, featuring a wine bar, open barista and fireplace. Haverson Architecture's solution positions the bars parallel to the long walls of the long, narrow and tall volume to connect each floor's front and back, punctuates its spatial confines with mezzanine openings, and immerses guests in a warm, well ordered and handsomely detailed evocation of Provence. Indeed, the blending of barn beams, knotty-pine trim, Venetian plaster, luxurious fabrics, bistro furniture and wall-length banquette downstairs, plush lounge furnishings upstairs, Provence-themed art and artifacts, color scheme of terracotta, marigold and clay, and romantic lighting design, provides a perfectly seasoned space for Bistro du Midi's seafood-oriented menu. In this milieu, even proper Bostonians are happily surrendering to the joys of marinated bay scallops, shellfish bouillabaisse and Pissaladiere, a flavorful Provencal tart.

*A: Bistro dining room   B: Private dining room
C: Upstairs dining room with wine bar and fireplace   D: Storefront and outdoor café
E: Bistro bar*
Photography: *Peter Paige*

HAVERSON ARCHITECTURE   Morello | Greenwich, Connecticut

Just by leasing the store at 253 Greenwich Avenue in Greenwich, Connecticut, Morello Bistro identified itself with a lofty, vaulted landmark interior designed by Rafael Guastavino Jr., son of the Catalan architect who created the famed, eponymous tile that lines vaulted ceilings, arches and columns. But a space where restaurants have come and gone provides no guarantees. To attract residents of historic and affluent Greenwich, restaurateur Marlon Abela asked Haverson Architecture to rethink the 1,650-square-foot interior of his new, 130-seat venue. The design team wisely made respectful adjustments to a space previous tenants often fought, relocating the bar to unify the long and narrow lower level, enhancing the mezzanines at front and back as distinctive settings, widening storefront window openings, and accentuating the stately architecture Guastavino originally conceived for a bank. The new environment has been praised for contrasting timeless architecture with warm, rich colors and elegant contemporary furnishings while using lighting to dramatize details and reinforce a sense of scale. Not only is Morello hailed by *Connecticut* Magazine as one of the "25 Most Romantic Restaurants in Connecticut," guests appreciate its gracious service and bistro fare such as rack of lamb, tagliatelle verde and osso buco Milanese.

A: Mezzanine   B: Bar   C: Storefront   D: Main dining room
Photography: *Peter Paige*

Off-price shopping centers have been part of the retail scene for years, and their increasingly attractive facilities illustrate how much they have shed their modest, no-frills roots in favor of a more mainstream image. At Tanger Mall, a 735,000-square-foot retail outlet center in Riverhead, New York featuring high-end brands, Haverson Architecture has designed a 96-seat, 4,000-square-foot Food Court that transforms a standard retail amenity into an upscale destination space. The new Food Court houses four food service concepts, including Wok & Roll (Asian), Nathan's (hotdogs and hamburgers), Famous Famiglia (Italian) and Grand Café Express (a new, custom concept). While the radial organization of the sleek, contemporary space places guest seating in the center, surrounded by concentric rings holding the circulation corridor, retail stores for the four concepts, and their kitchens, the four

concepts are the design's obvious focus. The Food Court balances its diverse elements with skill and care, nevertheless, giving each concept an image that stands out while reinforcing the harmony of the overall space. Its upscale interior of wood, tile, stone and solid surfacing, modern furnishings, and a stylish lighting scheme using fabric-covered pendant drum fixtures to highlight the radial layout quietly raises the stakes in off-price retailing.

A: Retail store   B: Entrance from parking
C: Guest seating and circulation corridor
Photography: *Wade Johnson*

Heitz Parsons Sadek

400 Clematis Street, Suite 203 • West Palm Beach, FL 33401 • 561.838.0033 • 561.650.7000 (Fax)

RM 612, Kuntai International Mansion Building 1 • Yi No.12 Chao Wai St. Chaoyang Dist. • Beijing 100020 China • 8610.5879.7555 • 8610.5879.7556 (Fax)

www.heitz-parsons-sadek.com

HEITZ PARSONS SADEK Hyatt Regency Jing Jin City | Tianjin, China

Built within an empty, existing structure, the Hyatt Regency Jing Jin City Resort and Spa, designed by Heitz Parsons Sadek, enables the 793-room luxury conference resort in Tianjin, China to satisfy every need of the city's Binhai New Area, a center of advanced industry, financial reform, and innovation where nearly 300 of the Fortune Global 500 companies maintain operations. Known for picturesque architecture that resembles an ancient, mythical royal palace surrounded by a labyrinth of pathways,

formal courtyards, lush gardens and natural geothermal hot springs, the Hyatt Regency is part of the 26-acre Jing Jin City mixed-use development. Thanks to new and upgraded spaces for its main lobby, tea lounge, pastry shop, four restaurants, junior and grand ballrooms, meeting facilities, spa, health club, guestrooms, suites, and the Hyatt Regency Club Hotel, a premium facility, the resort can readily play a growing role in local business and social affairs. Its facilities are clearly designed to stand out. The

lobby, for example, conjures a natural setting with its hand-painted dome, illuminated by softly changing lights, water sculpture, designed to please both eye and ear, and cozy seating groups, screened by fabric panels, finished in hewn limestone, chiseled

A: Main lobby, fountain B: Children's swimming pool C: Glass House Buffet, entrance D: Main lobby, registration
Photography: *Sun Xiang Yun*

HEITZ PARSONS SADEK

hardwood, end-cut solid oak and patinated copper panels, and furnished with stylish yet comfortable contemporary furniture. A very different mood prevails in the Glass House, an Asian-themed buffet restaurant. Here, buffet stations recreate the bustling ambiance of a local food market through themed pavilions, with the Beijing kitchen clad in traditional gray brick set in stacks, the Cantonese noodle stand featuring distressed wood, and the Japanese sushi bar combining bamboo and golden onyx. Perhaps the Garden Chinese Restaurant, an elegant restaurant inspired by the traditional Beijing hutong or rowhouse neighborhood, best demonstrates the new capabilities. Visually complex, the restaurant leads guests through interior corridors and courtyards en route to their dining quarters; starting with the entry foyer, where a shadow screen blocks the way to bad spirits, and walls are lined with sleek bands of hammered and polished black granite, continues with courtyard dining; brick-paved expanses where guests take their places at garden type seating for family-style dining; and concludes with VIP dining facilities that evoke a luxurious Chinese residence, with each dining room featuring an outdoor-like foyer, a mini-courtyard, and an elegant dining hall screened from the courtyard. For guests and visitors alike, traditional and modern China blend harmoniously at Hyatt Regency Jing Jin City.

A: The Garden, main entrance B: The Garden, garden family-style dining C: The Garden, VIP Dining D: Glass House Buffet, food stations and dining area E: Glass House Buffet, main dining

E

Close to the commercial heart of Muscat, the capital of the Sultanate of Oman on the Arabian Sea near the Straits of Hormuz, Al Bustan Palace InterContinental Muscat Hotel ushers guests into a main lobby of remarkable tranquility and elegance. The impressively tall space, bathed in the soft light of an oversized chandelier and domed ceiling and soothed by the sound of trickling water from a hand-blown glass fountain, is one of many interior environments designed by Heitz Parsons Sadek that gives the eight-story, 290-room Al Bustan Palace its notable feeling of refinement and comfort. Its modern-day design vocabulary, informed by the fundamentals of traditional Omani culture, is evident in such diverse facilities as four restaurants, ballroom, meeting rooms, business center, fitness center, wellness rooms and shopping arcade in addition to the lobby, 250 guestrooms, 40 executive suites—and 200 acres of private beach and lush green gardens featuring a

water sports center, Tennis Village and Al Bustan Palace Beach Club. Guests especially enjoy the hotel's cultural blend of past and present. State-of-the-art spaces come appointed in royal pearl hues with such timeless finishes as marble, gold leaf and hand-crafted wallcoverings and furniture, inspiring wonder as well as satisfaction.

A: Aerial view of hotel and grounds   B: Al Maha Piano Bar   C: Guestroom   D: Beach Pavilion Restaurant   E: Vue Restaurant F: Main lobby
***Photography:** V.S.M. Leonardo*

HEITZ PARSONS SADEK   Crowne Plaza New Delhi Okhla Hotel | New Delhi, India

Serving local and international information technology executives in New Delhi's emerging business hub at Okhla South Delhi is the primary focus of the new, 207-room, five-star Crowne Plaza New Delhi Okhla Hotel. It's a savvy move, considering that New Delhi, the capital of India, is one of the world's fastest growing cities, with a stake in the nation's rapidly expanding IT sector that is reshaping Okhla South Delhi. Yet the design has room for beauty and charm, thanks to a project team that included Heitz Parsons Sadek for space planning, FFE selection and purchasing, and construction document administration. Recognizing that a modern business environment provides style and comfort as well as efficiency, the client, Today Hotels, requested a modern environment enriched by Indian details. Thus, from the main lobby, ballroom, meeting facilities, spa, health club, shopping arcade and two fine-dining restaurants to guestrooms and suites, guests encounter clean, contemporary design tempered by warm, earthy colors, modern furnishings incorporating Indian motifs, and such timeless

materials as marble, carved plaster, wood and bronze. Another sign of the times: While one restaurant, Edesia, serves Indian and Western cuisine, Chao Bella offers adventurous guests an innovative fusion of Chinese and Italian cooking.

A: Guestroom   B: Chao Bella   C: Main lobby
Photography: TO BE IDENTIFIED

C

HEITZ PARSONS SADEK   Shangri-La Hotel | Xian, China

The new 390-room Shangri-La Hotel designed by Heitz Parsons Sadek is situated in the recently developed Gaoxin urban area of Xian. Xian is renowned as one of the Four Great Ancient Capitals of China, the eastern terminus of the Silk Road, and the home of the legendary Terracotta Army. Yet the city also thrives as a modern cultural, industrial and educational center, intensely involved in telecommunications, aerospace and software. As the only high-end hotel in Xian's Gaoxin high-tech development zone, the revitalized Shangri-La is more compelling than ever, as shown by its All Day Dining Café, Presidential and Shangri-La Suites, Executive Lounge, Spa, Infinity Pool and Health Club. Discreet and soothing, the Infinity Pool is an airy and elegant retreat caressed by soft lighting and the sound of trickling water. The unique sense of place in the Yi Café, an all-day dining restaurant, comes from the interplay between show kitchen and raised dining areas. As for the Presidential Suite, its luxurious ambiance contrasts the modern, ergonomic comfort of its seating with superbly detailed decorative furnishings. Room by room, Shangri-La is helping 3,100-year-old Xian act its age with style and substance.

A: *Shangri La Spa* *B:* *Yi Café* *C:* *Presidential Suite living room* *D:* *Presidential Suite study* *E:* *Infinity Pool*
Photography: *Sun Xiang Yun*

Heitz Parsons Sadek Jingya Huangsi Ocean Restaurant | Beijing, China

Trendy, upscale visitors and residents of Beijing are heading to the Jingya Ocean Entertainment Center, located only a few blocks from the Forbidden City, to explore the boldly expressive architecture as well as the entertainment center, restaurants, commercial space, meeting spaces, theater and exhibition space housed within the 10-floor, 120,000-square-foot structure. Here, Jingya Huangsi Ocean Restaurant, designed by Heitz Parsons Sadek, fulfills public expectation for an escapist experience by casting itself as a fantastic, contemporary design folly, an architectural interpretation of the beauties hidden in the underwater world, where fabulous seafood is served. The floor plan for the 124-table, 914-seat space consists of a main dining buffet restaurant and private dining rooms. While the restaurant's lobby and main dining room have a neutral, sandy color scheme, the private dining rooms are individually treated to their own identity, detailing, size and shape. The result is as much a work of stagecraft as it is interior design, evoking ocean life with organic forms and colors with such materials as terrazzo, custom fabricated glass, stainless steel and carved stone. Winning the patronage of a young, affluent and adventurous crowd is never easy, but this design clearly has them hooked.

A: Art gallery B: Atrium and feature staircase
C: Private dining room corridor D: Ten-person private dining room E: Twelve-person private dining room F: Main lobby
***Photography:** Sun Xiang Yun*

HEITZ PARSONS SADEK   Garden Court All Day Dining | Hua Ting Hotel & Towers | Shanghai, China

To prepare for its role as the five-star official reception hotel for Shanghai's highly successful Expo 2010, the 780-room Hua Ting Hotel & Towers embarked on a refurbishment program to ensure that its public facilities would meet the demands of world's fair visitors and sponsors as well as global media representatives. One of the most popular spaces developed for Expo 2010 that continues to enjoy steady patronage is the Garden Court All Day Dining, a 79-table, 246-seat restaurant, designed by Heitz Parsons Sadek, that is located beside the hotel lobby. Chef Michael Schauss's acclaimed international buffet is served in a sleek, contemporary interpretation of the traditional Chinese concept of "Light and Shadow." The design articulates positive and negative spaces by combining ancient gray ceramic roof tiles with semi-transparent, laminated glass panels and custom-designed pendant lighting fixtures, producing interiors that are stylish and modern yet reassuringly solid and tangible. Interestingly, the Garden Court's interactive food stations, arrayed throughout the main dining room (a private dining room is also available), work equally well for the general public and for event planners, inviting guests to explore a delectable world's fair of cuisines in Heitz Parsons Sadek's dynamic setting of "Light and Shadow."

A: Private dining room   B: Main dining room
Photography: *Sun Xiang Yun*

HEITZ PARSONS SADEK   Shanghai Spring Restaurant | Shanghai, China

Shanghai's famous Bund, the stately promenade of 19th- and early 20th-century European-style buildings lining the Huangpu River, projects a fresh and unfamiliar image when seen from the new, 98-table, 526-seat (plus 70 outdoor) Shanghai Spring Restaurant, designed by Heitz Parsons Sadek. That's because the restaurant sits atop the Super Brand Mall, a posh shopping center in Pudong, the dynamic high-rise district on the opposite bank of the river from the Bund. By day, when the masonry of the Bund is revealed in all its glory, or by night, when the façades glow with dramatic architectural lighting, the views are spectacular. In fact, the restaurant functions as a vitrine to display the architecture of this metropolis of 13 million residents, providing views of the historic waterfront from the main dining room, riverside dining room and even private dining rooms, which are enclosed with clear glass partitions and raised several steps for this purpose. Yet Shanghai Spring is a visual feast on its own, designed in a clean, contemporary style, finely crafted in Zebrano wood, red slump glass panels and marble, and furnished with sleek banquettes, tables, chairs and lighting fixtures as a worthwhile picture frame for an impressive view.

A: Main dining   B: Riverside dining and private dining room entrances   C: Riverside dining
Photography: *Sun Xiang Yun*

HEITZ PARSONS SADEK   Diaoyutai State Guesthouse & Conference Center | Beijing, China

Located on beautiful Yuyuantai Lake in the heart of Beijing, Diaoyutai State Guesthouse & Conference Center plays host to heads of state and other foreign dignitaries, captains of industry and international celebrities when they visit China, providing lodging and other services within the equivalent of a five-star, 203-room hotel. The facility, comprising 18 distinct buildings, incorporates such facilities as an indoor swimming pool, indoor tennis courts, bowling lanes, exercise rooms, spa, beauty parlor, 200-seat restaurant and eight banquet halls of varying sizes in addition to appropriately spacious, luxurious and comfortable guest

accommodations. Recently Diaoyutai added another vital element to its Camp David-like campus, the Conference Center, featuring an interior design won through an international competition by a winning team that included Heitz Parsons Sadek for space planning, FFE selection and specification, and construction documentation. A pairing of classic Chinese architecture with state-of-the-art equipment and technology, the Conference Center reflects the preference of the Ministry of Foreign Affairs for an environment that would be "grand without opulence, impressive without glitz, heroic without fanfare." Accordingly, the design is handled with dignity and restraint, merging a traditional approach to shapes, materials and colors with contemporary design concepts to welcome VIP guests to China.

A: Ballroom   B: Main lobby entrance
C: Ballroom chandelier
Photography: TO BE IDENTIFIED

HKS Hill Glazier Studio

1919 McKinney Avenue • Dallas, TX 75201 • 214.969.3379 • 214.969.3397 (Fax)

www.hksinc.com

Overlooking 24 mountainside and oceanfront acres at the southernmost tip of Mexico's Baja California Peninsula, Capella Pedregal is not only the premier spa resort in Cabo San Lucas, it is easily the most exclusive. The only way it can be reached is via a privately owned, 300-meter (984-foot) tunnel carved through the heart of the mountain separating the town of Cabo from the Pacific Ocean. The upscale resort, master planned and designed by HKS Hill Glazier Studio, creates a memorable guest experience by skillfully integrating its 66-suite hotel, 31 fractional-ownership units (Residences), 20 whole-ownership homes (Casonas), and such on-site services as a spa, fitness center, salon, swimming pool, sundeck, and two restaurants with its distinctive, rugged site. A modern interpretation of Mexican vernacular architecture constructed chiefly with regional materials by local craftsmen, Capella Pedregal appeals to affluent couples and families by creating minimal visual impact and harmonizing with the environment at the same time it provides an exceptional, residential-style environment. While excellent shopping, dining and entertainment are all within easy reach by foot, bike or car in nearby Cabo San Lucas, it's easy to see why residents and guests insist Capella Pedregal is truly a magical world apart.

A: Terrace with fire pit   B: Casita living room
C: Guestroom   D: Pool   E: Entry with fire pit
F: Seaside Grill
Photography: *Richard Holland/Robert Reck Photography*

You keep expecting a limousine to deliver Cary Grant, Joan Crawford or Clark Gable to the Montage Beverly Hills, so faithful is this 201-room luxury hotel (including 55 suites and 20 condominiums) to the architecture of the Spanish Colonial Revival and Mediterranean styles that defined greater Los Angeles in the 1920s and 1930s. However, the Montage Beverly Hills is brand new. Designed by HKS Hill Glazier Studio, architect, Darrell Schmitt Design Associates, interior designer, and Nancy Goslee Power and Associates, landscape architect, the hotel evokes Hollywood's Golden Age by dressing its modern-day setting, complete with a spa, rooftop pool and cabanas, meeting and event facilities, business center, retail stores and restaurants, in the arches, courtyards, plaster wall surfaces and terracotta tile roofs of that glamorous era. Yet the hotel is not content to pamper its guests. Working with the City of Beverly Hills, the sustainable, LEED-Gold hotel is also revitalizing the Golden Triangle district with an adaptive reuse project encompassing a 30,000-square-foot public garden—a first for the district—a 27,000-square-foot, city-owned commercial building adjacent to the hotel that generates rent for the municipality, and a four-level parking structure directly beneath the hotel, public garden and commercial building. Now that's a class act.

A: Spa entrance B: Rooftop pool C: Courtyard
D: Exterior with public garden E: Guestroom
F: Main entrance
Photography: *Scott Frances*

HKS Hill Glazier Studio   Tucker's Point Hotel & Spa | Harrington Sound, Bermuda

Bermuda's first all-new resort in nearly four decades, Tucker's Point Hotel & Spa is a traditional, Bermuda-style hotel in Harrington Sound, designed by HKS Hill Glazier Studio, that manages to be simultaneously contemporary and timeless. Providing the latest comforts and luxuries while respecting Bermuda's British Colonial culture, the 88-key hotel is the crown jewel of the Tucker's Point Club development. Its 200-acre site is spectacularly planned, beginning with the palm-lined drive overlooking the championship golf course and Castle Islands that takes guests to the residential-scaled lobby and stately, 52-key Manor House, and concluding with three additional guestroom buildings clustered like a hillside village on a slope descending to Castle Harbour. Rooms are sumptuous, ranging from 520-square-foot guestrooms to the 1,650-square-foot Governor's Suite, all equipped with five-fixture baths and terraces with breathtaking views. Of course, countless amenities exist to lure guests from their rooms, such as the spa, fitness center, conference center, Beach Club and swimming pools, golf clubhouse and course, and restaurants and bars. What pleases guests as well is the design's attention to detail. From full-service locker rooms at the golf clubhouse to the walking stick and butterfly net by each guestroom's door, nothing is left to chance.

A: Palm Court B: Fountain Pool C: Tucker's Point Golf Clubhouse D: Guestroom E: Stair in Manor House F: Manor House and Castle Harbour
Photography: *HKS/Blake Marvin (A, B, F); Courtesy of Tucker's Point Hotel & Spa (C, D, E)*

HKS Hill Glazier Studio   Rosewood Sand Hill | Menlo Park, California

The rich heritage of the relaxed California adobe vernacular is the inspiration for the Rosewood Sand Hill, a hotel and office development in Menlo Park, California, designed by HKS Hill Glazier Studio, architect, and BAMO, interior designer, making the casually elegant, 123-room hotel ideal for a wide array of guests. The hotel and the 100,000-square-foot office complex that shares its 21-acre site incorporate similar aspects of the California ranch tradition, including deep overhangs, low pitch roofs, deep recesses within thick walls, long, wide verandas and naturalistic landscaping. Not only do these elements optimize outdoor space, circulation, views and natural lighting, they enable the hotel to bring the outdoors inside. Thus, hotel guests are housed in 13 two-story cottages that surround six connected courtyards, occupying rooms ranging in size from a 527-square-foot Deluxe Room to a 2,372-square-foot, two-bedroom Presidential Villa and enjoying spectacular views from private balconies or terraces of the hotel's gardens, courtyards, and outdoor pool or the Santa Cruz Mountains. Demonstrating the synergy of the development, hotel guests and office tenants alike enjoy access to the hotel's restaurant, bar, meeting and banquet spaces, and spa, just minutes from the venture capital firms, businesses, and Stanford University.

A: Pool   B: Guest cottages and gardens
C: Entrance
Photography: HKS/Blake Marvin

ILLUMINATING CONCEPTS

First among luxury casino resorts to locate in a major American metropolis outside of Las Vegas, the 400-room MGM Grand Detroit has firmly established itself as Detroit's premiere gaming and hospitality destination. The task of combining Las Vegas glamour while paying homage to Detroit's architectural equity was presented to a prestigious design team consisting of Hamilton Anderson Associates in joint venture with SmithGroup, Cleo Design, Carol Harris, Lawrence Lee, Toni Chi, Super Potato and Illuminating Concepts. The award-winning design celebrates contemporary architectural detailing and memorably opulent interiors that salute its Motown heritage with Art Deco motifs and high quality materials, finishes and furnishings. Illuminating Concepts' lighting design brings those textures and experiences vibrantly to life, brilliantly complementing the spaces and activities it serves.

From the spectacular exterior façade lighting to the exposed filaments in the custom-designed chandeliers that highlight the unique mosaic ceiling in the Saltwater restaurant, every component of Illuminating Concepts' comprehensive lighting design reflects not only an extraordinary attention to detail, but a sophisticated understanding of how to integrate the visual with the experiential.

A: Hotel Lobby   B: Ignite Sushi Bar & Lounge C: Saltwater Seafood   D: Agua Rum & Tequila Bar   E: Exterior façade **Photography:** *Beth Singer Photography*

Fresh from a $200 million renovation design collaboration between The Ferchill Group/ Westin® and Kaczmar Architects, Forrest Perkins, Sandvick Architects, Harris Design Group together with Illuminating Concepts, the magnificent Westin Book Cadillac—grand dame of Detroit's Washington Boulevard—has reclaimed its prominence as Detroit's premiere hotel. The revitalized landmark now boasts 453 suites, over 60 residences and some of the Midwest's most dramatic public event spaces. Illuminating Concepts' sophisticated lighting design for the iconic Motown destination elegantly introduces modern-day lighting into a historical context. The plan combines period-style decorative elements with state-of-the-art architectural fixtures, accentuating a design that carefully preserves the essence of the Louis Kamper-designed 1924 Italian Renaissance structure and resonates with comfort and timeless character. Seamless integration between historical features and state-of-the-art lighting technology helps establish a lively balance between the splendor (that Presidents Truman, Eisenhower and Kennedy, Dr. Martin Luther King, Babe Ruth and Frank Sinatra experienced firsthand) and the practical, technology-driven demands of 21st-century life. The result is a restoration project worthy of the building that was both the world's tallest hotel and Detroit's hottest society destination when opened in 1924. From carefully concealed exterior lighting to breathtaking period chandeliers in the reimagined Venetian Ballroom, the Westin Book Cadillac is a technical, visual and artistic masterpiece.

A: Motor Bar   B: Exterior façade
C: Venetian Ballroom   D: Woodward Ballroom
Photography: *Kaczmar Architects*

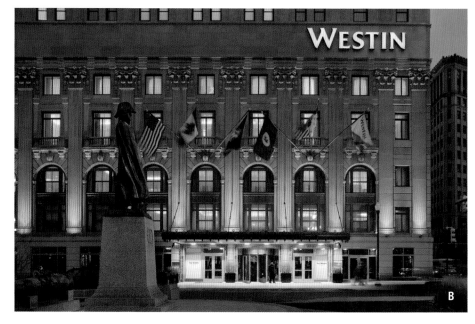

D

ILLUMINATING CONCEPTS   Rivers Casino | Pittsburgh, Pennsylvania

Rising over Pittsburgh's North Shore adjacent to Heinz Field, Rivers Casino displays a dazzling array of almost 3,000 slot machines, 86 table games, nine distinctive restaurants and bars, and a 1,000-seat riverside amphitheater against a backdrop of stunning views of the Ohio River and the Pittsburgh skyline. Working with local design architect Strada and master architect Bergman Walls & Associates, Illuminating Concepts designed and coordinated all lighting and A/V requirements to ensure the $410 million 130,973-square-foot casino would not only be a spectacular and iconic new addition to the revitalized riverfront, but would provide a unique multi-sensory guest experience. An illuminated exterior boardwalk promenade creates a literal and figurative connection with the waterfront, while the innovative and distinctive kinetic color-changing lighting treatments reflect the energy and vitality of the casino's contemporary glass, masonry and metal exterior and sleek, high-style interior. The multi-story cylindrical Drum Bar—both a central gathering point and vertical circulation zone—is subsequently transformed from a glass-enclosed vista for panoramic views by day into the star attraction in a spectacular nighttime sound and light show. It is the defining feature in a dynamic visual identity that enables Rivers Casino to show itself in what is literally a whole new light.

A: Blue light scene of River Casino's Drum Feature   B: Red light scene of River Casino's Drum Feature   C: Exterior façade
Photography: *Brad Feinknopf*

Located within the newly completed Rivers Casino in downtown Pittsburgh, the Wheelhouse is a modern sports lounge that provides the relaxing atmosphere of a high-end lounge with all the amenities of a "state of the art" sports bar. Philadelphia based Floss Barber, master architect Bergman Walls & Associates and IC collaborated on this exciting addition to the already widely successful Rivers Casino. IC provided the lighting and A/V design including the multipurpose stage environment that allows the Wheelhouse to flex between live acts, dance, and a sports broadcast facility to serve the lively sports crowd in Pittsburgh. The stage design culminates in a 15 ft. x 8 ft. HD LCD display that raises and lowers out of the ceiling to provide a wide range of options for viewing up to 12 games simultaneously or can be combined to display a single game across the entire screen.

A: Entrance   B: Giant LCD video display and viewing area   C: Bar   D: Lounge
Photography: *Brad Feinknopf*

ILLUMINATING CONCEPTS   Pure Nightclub | Las Vegas, Nevada

The super chic Pure Nightclub at Caesar's Palace is not only the largest nightclub in Las Vegas; it is also the world's first true ultra-lounge. The spectacular lighting concepts on display at Pure do more than just complement the architecture; they are the architecture. Illuminating Concepts' visionary lighting design, together with architectural and interior design by Bergman Walls & Associates and Avery Brooks & Associates, channels the essence of Miami's South Beach with vibrant tones of light played across elegant white drapes throughout airy, open volumes of space. The result is a showstopper: a truly unique and completely immersive environment and a skillful application of lighting design. A luminous palette of multicolored and multi-textured theatrical lighting activates the built environment and provides a distinctive visual and experiential identity to each of the club's main areas. The ultra-chic, 36,000-square-foot multistory club is comprised of three different areas: the pulsating main dance floor, the luxuriously private Red Room, and the spacious 14,000-square-foot outdoor Terrace with breathtaking views of the glittering Las Vegas Strip below.

A: Main Floor Bar   B: Red Room
Photography: *Bergman Walls & Associates*

Intra-Spec, Inc.

4218 Glencoe Avenue, Studio 1 • Marina Del Rey, CA 90292 • 310.821.0376 • 310.821.7151 (Fax)

www.intra-spec.com

Intra-Spec, Inc.   Laguna Cliffs Marriott Resort & Spa | Dana Point, California

Perched on cliffs overlooking the Pacific Ocean in southern California's scenic Dana Point, the four-story, 288,813-square-foot, 378-room Laguna Cliffs Marriott Resort & Spa, resplendent in its classic, red-roofed, Victorian-era architecture, is favored by business travelers and vacationers alike for its proximity to Orange County's corporate community, such attractions as Dana Point Harbor, Salt Creek Beach Park and Ocean Institute, and John Wayne Airport. Now, following an award-winning renovation, designed by Intra-Spec Hospitality Design, involving the lobby, guestrooms, suites, ballroom, OverVue

Lounge and Deck, meeting areas, corridors, Laguna and Del Mar Pools, and Kahuna Laguna Kids Club, the hotel has modernized its look and feel while retaining and enhancing its heritage. Not only are public spaces reconfigured to conform to current codes and promote flow, continuity and openness, interiors are infused with fresh colors, textures and forms inspired by the sea, such modern conveniences as LCD televisions, Wi-Fi, and iPod- and iPhone-ready connections, and such timeless, high quality materials as limestone, glass mosaics, mother of pearl, mahogany, limed oak, chrome, leather,

chenille, Axminster carpet and elegant lighting. Guests seeking bustling spaces for socializing or serene areas for contemplation will find them here—surrounded by breathtaking perspectives of the Pacific Ocean.

A: OverVue Lounge   B: Bar at OverVue Lounge
C: Reception Lobby   D: Conceirge desk
E: Lobby Lounge Fireplace   F: Guest bedroom
G: OverVue Deck   H: Presidential Suite
Photography: *Ben Carufel/InSite Architectural Photography*

INTRA-SPEC, INC.   The Langham Huntington Hotel and Spa | Pasadena, California

Hollywood was an orange grove in 1907, when the fabled 380-room Langham Huntington began welcoming guests to nearby Pasadena. A century later, the hotel offers everything from majestic interiors that include a Michelin Star restaurant, top-rated spa, three ballrooms and other facilities for meetings, events and weddings encompassing over 50,000 square feet, to 23 acres of formal gardens, tennis courts, outdoor pool and unique guest cottages. To update its timeless elegance for VIPs—including movie stars seeking a hideaway minutes from Los Angeles—the hotel recently completed a sparkling renovation, designed by Intra-Spec Hospitality Design, that brings new stylistic cohesion to public and guest spaces while embellishing their individual character. The renovation employs classic, Regency-inspired furnishings and fabrics in sophisticated finishes, patterns and colors to give a fresh look to interiors, combining modern convenience with Old World spaciousness, opulence and comfort. Thus, guests can indulge themselves in luxurious spaces appointed in walnut, marble, velvets, silk, handmade area rugs and axminster carpet that are saturated in hues ranging from light gold, rose and cerulean blue to hunter green, crimson and royal blue. If they desire broadband Internet access along with Afternoon Tea in the Lobby Lounge, the Langham Huntington will happily oblige.

A: Tea Room   B: Tournament of Roses Suite
C: Guest Bedroom   D: Georgian Ballroom
E: Bar
Photography: *Courtesy of Langham Hotels International*

INTRA-SPEC, INC. Sheraton Universal Hotel | Universal City, California

Although America's filmmakers began migrating from New York to Los Angeles as early as 1910, the Sheraton Universal Hotel, in Universal City, became the "Hotel of the Stars" soon after opening in 1969, adroitly exploiting its proximity to Universal Studios, Hollywood and Beverly Hills. To encourage more entertainment industry gatherings in its public spaces, including the lobby, reception, lobby lounge, Sheraton Link Business Center, Californias Restaurant and Starview Room, the hotel has unveiled a dramatic renovation, designed by Intra-Spec Hospitality Design. The makeover embraces

Hollywood Glam, a style blending French Regency, Greek Revival and Art Deco, relocating the bar and giving it an approachable, elliptical shape, adding similar elliptical elements to the lounge and registration pods for continuity, and installing semi-private cabanas in the lobby lounge to introduce an indoor/outdoor feeling. Finishes and colors establish a crisp, clear mood, incorporating classic furnishings upholstered with luxury fabrics, a material palette of lacquer, tile, marble, mahogany, ebony, chrome and Murano glass, and a color scheme of black, white and silver with yellow and green

accents. To complete the facelift, the design adds nostalgic decorative elements from Hollywood's golden age that should make today's Freds and Gingers feel right at home.

A: Cabana Seating in Lobby Lounge
B: Lobby Bar C: Sheraton Link Business Center D: Reception E: Starview Room
F: Lobby Lounge Bar G: Lobby Lounge
Photography: *Jon Didier*

E

F

118

G

INTRA-SPEC, INC.   The Copley Square Hotel | Boston, Massachusetts

The first hotel to serve Boston's Back Bay when it opened on July 4, 1891, the 300-room Copley Square Hotel has emerged from a gracious renovation, designed by Intra-Spec Hospitality Design, that demonstrates how to update a landmark with small guestrooms and traditionally configured lobby. Major goals that drove the project, comprising the lobby, Xhale Restaurant, 1891 Meeting Room, guestrooms and corridors, were maximizing floor area, opening up space, modernizing layouts, introducing luxurious details and enhancing the hotel's heritage. Numerous techniques combine to achieve the award-winning results. Scaled down guestroom seating, for example, makes guestrooms seem larger. Similarly, a modern lobby layout featuring high-backed, wraparound banquettes encourages socializing; modernized classic furnishings and contemporary textiles and lighting bring immediacy and excitement to traditional décor; and custom wallcoverings with historical texts and framed, turn-of-the-century photographs keep the past accessible. Other ways the Copley Square embraces modernity include a material palette of black granite, chrome, oak, mahogany, leather, silk, velvet and flannel fabrics, a color scheme of slate gray, champagne, taupe, silver and cream accented by persimmon, and Wi-Fi, flat screen TVs, and MP3 players in each room—amenities former guests like William McKinley, Duke Ellington and Babe Ruth would surely have appreciated.

A: Reception B: Guestroom C: Xhale Restaurant D: Elevator Lobby
Photography: *Timothy Law/MBox Communications*

LIFESCAPES INTERNATIONAL

LIFESCAPES INTERNATIONAL   Encore at Wynn Las Vegas | Las Vegas, Nevada

Timing is everything in Las Vegas, as Steve Wynn knows. When Wynn opened the Wynn Las Vegas on April 28, 2005, it observed the 55th anniversary of the opening of the Desert Inn originally on the site. On April 28, 2006, the phenomenally successful upscale resort celebrated its first year by breaking ground on a second hotel, the Encore at Wynn Las Vegas, a $2.3 billion, 2,034-room tower adjacent to the existing resort and on the remaining Las Vegas Boulevard frontage. The architecture, designed by The Jerde Partnership in association with Butler/ Ashworth Architects, and the landscape, designed by Lifescapes International, declare that the Encore is uniquely different—more youthful, sophisticated and contemporary—from its parent. The 25-acre landscape shapes the Encore indoors and outdoors. Dramatic views from the casino onto the pool areas and through the exterior parterre gardens extend the spirit of the high-tech yet romantic interiors, which feature contemporary aesthetics infused with Asian motifs. Vistas from the restaurants and nightclubs towards the exterior, a European, adults-only pool, a main pool area with 29 private cabanas poolside, and Encore Beach Club (codesigned with Roger Thomas and his team), a lush oasis of hedonism, complete the landscape's upscale atmosphere.

A: Main pool area   B: Cabanas in main pool area   C: Parterre garden   D: Landscape outside casino   E: Pavilion with outdoor hearth   F: Encore Beach Club
Photography: *Eric Figge Photography and Owner Provided*

A

LIFESCAPES INTERNATIONAL   Wynn Las Vegas | Las Vegas, Nevada

Although Steve Wynn had won Las Vegas's respect for properties he developed, his first endeavor as Wynn Resorts had to be better. Fielding a stellar project team including Marnell Corrao Associates, architect, Roger Thomas, interior designer, Patrick Woodroffe, lighting designer, Lifescapes International, landscape architect, and Tom Fazio, golf course architect, he topped expectations for Wynn Las Vegas's award-winning, 2,716-room hotel and casino resort on 50 acres (plus Wynn Golf Course's 150 acres). Determined to internalize the experience of a Wynn destination, he worked with Lifescapes to turn the gardens inward and away from "the show" along the Las Vegas Strip. (Speaking to Julie Brinkerhoff-Jacobs, Lifescapes' president, Wynn insisted, "If people want to see what we're doing, they need to come inside and get fully engaged.") The landscape would richly reward guests. The 100-foot-high mountain, complete with hundreds of mature pines and cascading waterfalls, that

Lifescapes created for Wynn was an industry first. Also unique were elaborate pool areas with custom-crafted topiary arbors and private cabanas, sequestered dining areas with their own garden settings, set against mountain and lake, and interior atrium gardens and enclosed koi pond conservatory at the south entry. Today, a remarkable verdant signature is essential to Wynn Resorts everywhere.

A: Pool area   B: Floral planting bed
C: Outdoor dining   D: Cascading waterfalls
E: Garden   F: Hotel tower and landscape frontage
Photography: *Eric Figge Photography and Owner Provided*

F

LIFESCAPES INTERNATIONAL   Tao Beach | The Venetian | Las Vegas, Nevada

For guests who can't get enough of its DJ-driven Tao Nightclub, high above the Las Vegas Strip, The Venetian, the 4,027-room resort hotel and casino famed for replicating Italy's legendary city on the Adriatic Sea, now offers Tao Beach on the nightclub's roof. This 18,000-square-foot pool deck has been designed by Lifescapes International with interior designer Thomas Schoos Design and lighting designer Matthew Paupst as a Balinese-inspired outdoor oasis and nightclub. Instantly embraced by a young and fun-loving clientele, Tao Beach invites them to mingle day and night among swimming pools, cabanas, poolside lounges with day beds and chaise lounges, a DJ booth and a 30-foot bar, all surrounded by 40-foot-high bamboo trees, 14-foot-high fire columns and lush tropical horticulture. Careful detailing makes Tao Beach a crowd pleaser. Guests who reserve the luxury cabanas can expect such amenities as air conditioning, high definition plasma screen TVs with gaming consoles, WiFi and customized mini bars, while everyone else can revel in high energy music from a state-of-the-art sound system, food and beverage service from The Venetian's acclaimed Tao Asian Bistro, and a seductive setting where there's always a pool nearby when the action gets too hot.

A: Aerial view   B: Poolside cabanas
Photography: *Lifescapes International*

B

LIFESCAPES INTERNATIONAL   Hotels in Macao | Venetian Macao, Four Seasons Macao | Macao, China

Asia's stunning economic ascent can be measured in many ways, and the Venetian Macao and Four Seasons Macao are as good examples as any. The Venetian Macao, a Las Vegas Sands casino resort on the Cotai Strip in southern China's Macao, deliberately and decisively dwarfs its Las Vegas sibling. Its international design team, including Aedas, executive architect, HKS, lead design architect, and Lifescapes International, landscape architect, has created a 10.5 million-square-foot complex that features a replica of Venice's Grand Canal along with a 3,000-suite, 32-story hotel tower, 1.2 million-square-foot convention space, 1.6 million-square-foot retail space and 550,000-square-foot casino. Its superb, 150-acre landscape, encompassing thousands of mature trees, flowering shrubs and annual/perennial flowers, is Italian inspired but locally grown. Much more intimate in scale, the 360-room Four Seasons Macao nevertheless commands respect as a five-star hotel and the next property to open along the Cotai Strip after the Venetian Macao. Designed by Steelman Partners, architect, Hirsch Bedner Associates, interior designer, and Lifescapes International, landscape architect, it welcomes guests to a grand entry drive, five outdoor swimming pools, and an array of lush gardens supporting hand-picked gems of intricate, regionally appropriate foliage that guests have likened to a glimpse of heaven.

A: Entry courtyard, Four Seasons   B: Lake and gardens, Venetian Macao   C: Swimming pool cabanas, Venetian Macao   D: Grand Canal, Venetian Macao
Photography: *Lifescapes International*

Welcome to Italy's Lake Como as only Las Vegas could present it. A shimmering, 8-acre replica of the lake, animated by a brilliantly choreographed water-fountain-and-music extravaganza and ornamented by a charming representation of an Italian lakeside village, introduces you to Bellagio, MGM Mirage Resorts' 3,933-room, 4.8 million-square-foot luxury casino hotel resort. Though Bellagio was inspired by its Old World namesake, guests love its distinctive look and feel, created through a close collaboration between previous owner/developer Steve Wynn and a design team including Jerde Partnership International, Atlandia Design, and Lifescapes International, landscape architect. The resort's 65-acre Mediterranean garden setting is integral to the guest experience. Featuring over 1,300 trees, thousands of flowers and shrubs, hand-pruned trees among the outdoor pools, a landscaped lobby and an indoor conservatory famed for seasonal garden settings, the scheme also thoughtfully retains nearly 300 majestic pine trees and other plant materials from the previous golf course on the site. Despite all the seductive attractions that the Bellagio offers, the landscape consistently manages to lure crowds to savor its

lush plantings, a century-old fountain, and a serene atmosphere that would seem familiar to residents of the original Lake Como.

A: Aerial view of pool area   B: Hotel tower, lake and fountain   C: Indoor conservatory with Fourth of July setting
***Photography:** Eric Figge Photography*

The gaming industry in Atlantic City, New Jersey, took a deep breath in 2003 when The Borgata Hotel Casino & Spa bought Las Vegas-style high-end luxury to Renaissance Pointe, far from the legendary Boardwalk. Would the public embrace The Borgata's sleek, 2,000-room, 35-story hotel, spacious, 161,000-square-foot casino and other high-styled facilities for dining, entertainment and shopping? Now, its overnight success story has a sequel: The Water Club. Designed as an annex by a project team including Bower Lewis Thrower and Cope Linder Associates as design architects, Laurence Lee &

Associates as principal interior designer, and Lifescapes International as landscape architect for the interiors and pool, the 800-room, 43-story hotel offers a more luxurious and sophis- ticated environment than its older sibling. As The Borgata's original landscape architect, Lifescapes International was entrusted by the joint venture of Boyd Gaming Corporation and MGM Mirage Resorts to design a fun, trendy landscape environment that focused on an interior garden setting. The award-winning design solution establishes a dynamic balance between architecture and environment. Guests at

The Water Club experience a stylish, contemporary landscape where hand picked garden elements and superbly crafted sculptural plant selections establish an inviting cosmopolitan ambiance for The Water Club's 21st-century architecture and interior design.

A: Indoor swimming pool   *B:* Registration
C: Restaurant/lounge
Photography: *John Mini Distinctive Landscapes - Landscape Contractor*

LIFESCAPES INTERNATIONAL   Fairmont Newport Beach | Newport Beach, California

Even the finest hotels can emerge like Cinderella from a makeover, which is why the Fairmont Newport Beach, in Newport Beach, California (a Sunstone property), recently completed an extensive renovation designed by Lee & Sakahara Architects AIA, Inc., architect, Design Force Corporation, interior designer, and Lifescapes International, landscape architect. Mindful of the 440-room luxury hotel's prized role in the business and social life of affluent Orange County, Lifescapes International concentrated on elevating the image of specific areas, including the

outdoor swimming pool deck, restaurant, entries and gathering places, using landscaping to add beauty, dignity and charm. The once uneventful drive leading to the Fairmont's entrance, for example, has now reemerged as a gorgeous procession of mature palms, majestic pines and rich swaths of seasonal color. Interiorscape and outdoor landscape has added to the cachet of the Bambú Restaurant for the business entertaining and weddings that fill the hotel's calendar of events. An outdoor terrace has been transformed into a verdant living room

without walls, thanks to outdoor furniture and plantings, inviting business and wedding planners to include it in their itineraries. Endowed with sun-drenched beaches, world-class shopping, and exciting nightlife, the "O.C." once again has a Fairmont Newport Beach worthy of its address.

A: Pool deck   B: Outdoor meeting area
C: Exterior showing entrance drive
Photography: *Owner Provided*

One of the first major casino resorts built off the Strip in Las Vegas developed by Station Casinos in recent years is Red Rock Casino, Resort & Spa, which engages its picturesque mountain setting in the suburb of Summerlin via a unique, contemporary sensibility. As a result, the 70-acre, 850-room luxury resort, designed by Friedmutter Group, architect, interior designer, Lifescapes International, landscape architect, Perini Construction Group, general contractor, and Kaplan Partners, lighting designer, projects a bold, modern image that complements the thriving, upscale community surrounding it. Red Rock's 14-acre landscape environment invites hotel guests and local residents to explore and experience its numerous destination "gardens within gardens." Building on formal geometric patterns, drought-tolerant plant materials and carefully balanced textures and colors, the landscape dramatizes key entry points and transition areas to reward the

discovery-seeking visitor at every turn. Preceding the entry to the casino, for example, is a stunning, black-tiled, tiered waterfall illuminated by fire bowls. Clusters of tornado palms, bordering a dancing ornamental pond, soar 40 feet into the air to frame the hotel's entrance. The main pool area's dramatic "of the moment" design lets guests "be seen" or "not be seen." Don Brinkerhoff, FASLA/CEO of Lifescapes, declares Red Rock "a place of continuous discovery."

A: Main pool B: Fountain at main pool
C: Aerial view of main pool D: Cherry Nightclub
E: Sign fountain at entrance F: One of many "gardens within gardens" G: Robert Indiana's "LOVE" sculpture
***Photography:** Lifescapes International*

LIFESCAPES INTERNATIONAL   Fontainebleau Resort | Miami Beach, Florida

An icon of Miami hospitality originally designed by architect Morris Lapidus with owners Turnberry Associates and completed in 1954, the Fontainebleau Resort recently received an inspired renovation designed by Nichols Brosch Wurst Wolfe & Associates, design architect, HKS, Inc., executive architect, Jeffrey Beers International, interior design/interface with select landscape areas, and Lifescapes International, landscape architect. Balancing contemporary design and historic elements, the project allows guests of the 8.9-acre, 1,504-room hotel to revel in legendary settings while experiencing modern conveniences and comforts. The landscape design introduces such desirable features as the Main Pool, a four-foot-deep private pool with rim flow, pool bar and main cabanas with private lawns, Ultra-Lounge Pool, a club-like setting where VIP cabanas overlook pools, the Round Pool, a pool with center "floating" island, rim flow and party cabana, and the Kid's Pool, an 18-inch pool and play area with cabanas for parents. The firm incorporated Lapidus' "bowtie" design while shaping the pools and waterways, honoring an earlier era while creating a modern environment to satisfy today's guests. Its successful design composition honors Fontainebleau's rich heritage with a tropical flora environment reprised with coconut palms, philodendrons, foxtail palms and bougainvillea, laying a solid yet spectacular foundation for the hotel's next half century.

A: Ultra Lounge Pool bar and VIP cabanas
B: Hotel and landscape   *C:* Aerial view of water features
Photography: *Lifescapes International*

LIFESCAPES INTERNATIONAL Hotels in Thailand | Diamond Cliff, Patong, Thailand | Thavorn Bay Resort, Phuket, Thailand

A: Thavorn Bay Resort *B: Diamond Cliff Resort*
Photography: *Owner Provided*

Steeply sloping sites can stop the most determined real estate developers. For two hotel resorts in Thailand, however, Lifescapes International has spectacularly demonstrated landscape architecture's power to turn this potential liability into a signature asset. For the 200-room (plus villas) Diamond Cliff Resort, in Patong, taming the incline from the hilltop entrance to the Andaman Sea and white sand Kalim Beach was compounded by the need to

create the impression of a secluded resort on a 20-acre site just minutes from downtown. Lifescapes International planted variegated greens, breezy, majestic palms and other locally grown native trees, along with colorful, blooming shrubs and flowers, to create a dense jungle tapestry along carefully crafted walkways, transforming the hillside into a must-see for guests. At the 195-room (plus villas and bungalows) Thavorn Bay Resort, in Phuket, the

dramatic cascade from the summit to Nakalay Bay was both the problem and the solution to making its remote, 25-acre site unique among competing local resorts. Romantic tropical gardens, each distinctive and unforgettable in its own design, and a picturesque, freeform swimming pool let guests pause in their descent through the lushly forested hillside, take in the spectacle, and rave about it to family and friends.

Lighting Design Alliance

2830 Temple Avenue • Long Beach, CA 90806 • 562.989.3843 • 562.989.3847 (Fax)

Two North Riverside Plaza, Suite 1475 • Chicago, IL 60606 • 312.441.1426 • 312.993.0167 (Fax)

PO Box 14564 • Dubai, UAE • 971.50.6456021 • 971.4.2714257 (Fax)

3270 Belmont Court • Wellington, CO 80549 • 970.219.8624

www.lightingdesignalliance.com

LIGHTING DESIGN ALLIANCE Atlantis Paradise Island | Phase III Expansion | Paradise Island, Nassau, Bahamas

The mythological Atlantis may have inspired Atlantis Paradise Island in Nassau, The Bahamas, but imaginative design, quality construction and world class service have built the sprawling hotel and casino into one of the world's largest and most popular resorts. Its Phase III expansion delivers over one million square feet of new facilities, featuring two 21-story towers—a 600-suite, all-suite hotel and 500-room condominium hotel, both featuring architecture by WATG and HKS Architects with interiors by Hirsch Bedner Associates and Jeffrey Beers International—a shopping mall, multi-pool outdoor patio and water park. Lighting Design Alliance's lighting scheme is essential to Phase III. Not only is lighting critical to the design, so are its energy consumption, construction and materials. For example, because island energy costs are triple those in mainland locations, energy-efficient lighting prevails throughout the project, such as the exclusive use of infrared halogen lamps and compact fluorescent fill lights in all guest rooms and residences. Numerous facilities are partly enclosed, requiring interior lighting capable of withstanding extreme winds and water. Finally, to counter corrosion caused by the Caribbean Sea's

salty, humid air, exterior light fixtures are specified in high-grade stainless steel or anodized aluminum with a powder coat paint finish.

*A: Pool cabana bar **B:** Lounge **C:** Spa entry*
***D:** Outdoor patio **E:** Registration **F:** Exterior pool deck*
***Photography:** © Atlantis Digital Asset Library*

LIGHTING DESIGN ALLIANCE Beijing Noodle Company No.9 | Caesars Palace | Las Vegas, Nevada

Casual noodle shops populate the streets of Shanghai, Hong Kong and Beijing, serving the traditional soup, dim sum, noodle and rice dishes that executive chef Li Yu of Beijing Noodle Company No. 9, at Caesar's Palace, in Las Vegas, prepares along with his own specialties. But there's nothing commonplace or traditional about the 3,500-square-foot restaurant. Designed by Bergman, Walls & Associates, architect, Design Spirits, interior designer, and Lighting Design Alliance, lighting designer, this multi-layered, cocoon-like environment of pattern and light—all white except for the food, place settings and goldfish in giant tanks flanking the entrance—projects an image that is dazzling, disconcerting and hypnotic. Lighting defines Beijing Noodle in various ways. LED tapelights on the back of wall- and ceiling-mounted metal screens pierced in custom patterns emit a warm glow that can be adjusted for lunch and dinner settings. PAR20 halogen trackheads positioned between screens spotlight tables and fish tanks, bringing out the vibrant colors of table settings and goldfish. Surface-mounted linear fluorescent striplights with T5 lamps add yet another layer of light by uplighting the food in the entry display kitchen and bar face at the back. The results are stunning for the food, people and space.

A: Bar B: Dining room C: Entry
D: Storefront
Photography: © *Kelly Stampa Gaez/KSG*
Photography

C

D

165

A city accustomed to erupting volcanoes and attacking pirates took notice in 1999 when a breathtaking evocation of Italy's majestic, water-borne Venice opened in Las Vegas to inaugurate the Venetian Resort, Hotel and Spa, designed by WATG as architect, Dougall Design Associates and KNA Interior Design as interior designer, Lifescapes International as landscape architect, and Lighting Design Alliance as lighting designer. The Venetian's main attraction was replicas of landmarks such as the Doge's Palace, Clock Tower, Campanile and Grand Canal. A decade after their debut, they still define the resort's upscale dining, shopping, casino and spa, all contained in a sprawling, low-rise

structure, and 4,027 guest rooms, housed in two high-rise towers. Creative lighting enhances their appeal. For example, to uplight the faux-sky ceiling above the 500,000- square-foot Grand Canal Shoppes, flickering lanterns create sparkle along pedestrian areas while concealed uplights wash the ceilings, reinforced by micro-sized accents integrated into themed façades to highlight architectural features. The scheme is sustainable too. As metal halide lamps in asymmetric fixtures provide an even wash of light on the ceiling that reduces energy and HVAC costs by 500 percent, specialized controls further cut energy costs and extend lamp life here and throughout America's "Venice." In 2010

Lighting Design Alliance was honored to update our original award winning design by retrofitting the lighting system to today's standards and efficiencies without sacrificing aesthetic. With an in-depth knowledge of the existing architecture and lighting system, as well as of sustainable lighting products, LDA's team is able to provide the top-end design specification recommendations to keep The Venetian a premier world destination.

*A: Grand Canal Shoppes **B:** Doge's Palace*
*C: Campanile and Hotel Tower **D:** Clock Tower, Doge's Palace and Lagoon*
Photography: *© RMA Architectural Photography*

Japanese chef Uechi Katsuya has produced a popular recipe for his Southern California restaurants by pairing his innovative cuisine—think of crispy rice with spicy tuna, Kobe filet with foie gras, and almond crusted scallops—with an equally creative environment, designed by French interior designer Philippe Starck with DesignARC as architect of record and Lighting Design Alliance as lighting designer. Starck's concept, developed by SBE Entertainment, turns three spaces in Los Angeles's Brentwood and Hollywood neighborhoods and one in Glendale into sleek, smooth and luminous wood bento boxes. Their only decorative elements are unforgettable: bold, mural-like backlit acrylic panels bearing mostly photographic images of the hands and facial features of geisha. Everything else is clean and unornamented, including wood wall and ceiling panels, glass vitrines on stone counters, plush fabric offset by sleek chrome, and concealed lighting fixtures visible only through their effects. To make the highly refined yet energy-efficient lighting possible, the design incorporates such details as

table accent downlights relamped and aimed from catwalks above the fixture housings, acrylic wall panels lit by single fluorescent strips using parabolic reflectors to span entire image heights, and various energy-efficient lamps. Chic young Angelenos apparently can't have enough of Katsuya by Starck.

A: Dining room/sushi bar (Hollywood)
B: Dragon Room (Hollywood) C: Dining room (Los Angeles) D: Private dining (Hollywood) E: Booth table (Los Angeles)
F: Sushi Bar (Glendale)
Photography: *© James Merrell (A, B, F), Skott Sinider/SBE Entertainment Group (C, E), Bryan Klammer (D)*

Because business and recreation commingle effortlessly in Orlando—where "children of all ages" can enjoy Disney World, Universal Studios, Sea World and Busch Gardens—the new, 1,400-room Hilton Orlando has been designed by HKS Architects as architect, Looney & Associates as interior designer, and Lighting Design Alliance as lighting designer to let guests enjoy both activities. In fact, the Hilton Orlando is directly linked via skybridge to the Orange County Convention Center to leverage its role as a meeting and convention hotel that doubles as a full-service resort and spa. Its full-scope lighting design reflects this, encompassing exterior lighting for the building façade, pool deck, sports courts, miniature golf course, driveways and parking areas, and interior lighting for all guest rooms, lobby, retail, spa, bars, restaurants, ballrooms and meeting rooms. Accordingly, the lighting scheme delivers practicality and sustainability along with utility and drama. For example, the façade's halo-like glowing frame showcases the building at night without flooding the entire exterior. Although fluorescent striplights wash up the top horizontal parapets, narrow spot floodlights equipped with metal halide lamps—studied to ensure compatibility of color and effect— are substituted for the corner vertical elements to simultaneously ease concerns of access for maintenance as they dazzle guests.

A: Exterior   B: Pool deck and lazy river
C: Ballroom prefunction   D: Boardroom
E: Ballroom   F: Lobby reception
Photography: © Ellen Cornell/Cornell & Company

Staples Center has given Los Angeles a legitimate reason to go downtown, and the sports and entertainment arena marked its 10th anniversary in 2009 with a $20 million renovation that made the journey even more rewarding. Providing amenities for before, during and after scheduled events, the makeover introduced a new luxury destination for A-list customers on the C-level: the Hyde Lounge, designed by the Studio Collective as interior designer and Lighting Design Alliance as lighting designer for a partnership formed by SBE Entertainment and Anschutz Entertainment Group. The 4,000-square-foot design projects a men's club ambiance while evoking its fabled Sunset Boulevard predecessor, combining eight premium suites into two salons, three bars, private "great room" and dance floor. To complement interiors featuring leather booths, rosewood and upholstered walls, ceilings of onyx, mirror and gold tile, floating LCD TV screens and state-of-the-art sound systems, the lighting scheme creates appropriate moods by highlighting design details. These include the backlit fluorescent onyx reveals in the leather booths, and casting selected areas in a seductive glow, as typified by the LED-backlit, tiled onyx ceiling above the dance floor, which alternates between even illumination during events and programmable, color-changing sequences when the action shifts upstairs.

A: Bar detail B: VIP lounge C: Dance floor
D: Bar E: Salon with leather booths
Photography: © SBE Entertainment

C

D

E

LIGHTING DESIGN ALLIANCE   The Cheesecake Factory | Multiple Locations

Beloved for its generous portions of over 200 tasty menu selections, imaginative and theatrical décor featuring French limestone floors and columns, hand-painted fabrics, cherry wood trim and dramatic lighting, friendly, energetic and well-trained staff, and legendary repertoire of 50 cheesecakes and desserts, The Cheesecake Factory has been pleasing guests since 1978, expanding from one restaurant in Beverly Hills to nearly 150 locations today. Lighting Design Alliance has designed lighting for up to 20 of the chain's restaurants each year since 2003, collaborating with the Architects Design Consortium and TRM Architecture, Design and Planning. The soft,

romantic lighting that characterizes The Cheesecake Factory's signature look requires multiple lights and strategies, incorporating table spots, wall accents, mural uplights, ceiling coves and concealed millwork lights, along with custom-made blown glass pendants and sconces. Since energy conservation is also important to The Cheesecake Factory, all its locations have dimmer systems designed to automatically adjust lights for time and sun location. In addition, Lighting Design Alliance spends several days at each new restaurant aiming lights and tuning dimmer settings, leaving The Cheesecake Factory's operations team to diligently monitor lamping, aiming and table placement and keep the facility looking its best for years to come.

A: Entry with bar   B: Dining room with booths and banquettes   C: Dessert counter D: Exterior
Photography: *© AG Photography, Anthony Gomez*

At the legendary corner of Hollywood and Vine in Hollywood where the Palace Theater once stood, the S Bar opened as an intimate neighborhood bar with a loft-like setting designed by DesignARC and French interior designer Philippe Starck, displaying an edgy blend of cultured sophistication and raw, youthful energy that made it an overnight sensation. Starck's chic and witty interior called for an equally whimsical lighting design and got one, designed by Lighting Design Alliance. Despite such undeniable follies as individualized table lamps suspended upside-down from the ceiling, the scheme was grounded in practicality. While fixture selection honored the owner's request for minimal lamp types and easy maintenance, energy consumption conformed to California's Title 24 energy code, with no lamp exceeding 41-watts VIA; three 7-watt candelabras illuminate the glowing shades; and

20-watt spots using infrared halogens providing punch to white tabletops. There was a touch of magic nonetheless—translucent imagery was projected on the drapery that enveloped the space, adding depth and shadows to accentuate the drapery's illusion that the space was much larger than it was. Of course, the overall design goal was to attract a young and stylish clientele, and full houses night after night proclaimed Hollywood's embrace of S Bar.

A: Bar   B: Table seating
Photography: *© SBE Entertainment Group/ James Merrell*

Marnell Architecture

222 Via Marnell Way • Las Vegas, NV 89119 • 702.739.2000 • 702.739.2005 (Fax)

www.marnellcompanies.com

Besides reigning as one of the world's top travel destinations, Las Vegas has also held the distinction of being one of America's fastest-growing metropolises, having evolved into a lucrative regional market of over two million residents. Creating a casino and resort especially for the people of Las Vegas, for whom the glittering spectacles on and off the Strip are everyday phenomena, presented a special challenge to the M Resort, in Henderson, Nevada, 10 miles south of the heart of the Strip. However, the recent completion of the 606,492-square-foot, 390-room casino and resort on a 93-acre site, designed by Marnell Architecture, ably demonstrates the power of design to serve the needs of a specific market. As its public space demonstrates, the M Resort targets local and out-of-town customers who appreciate value in lodging, dining, entertainment and other services.

It also demonstrates contemporary design that stresses timeless elegance over trendy ostentation—while offering every convenience and comfort visitors expect of Las Vegas resorts. The award-winning project has been master planned to allow for the full build-out of the site, where a 16-story hotel tower, two-story casino building enclosing a 90,000-square-foot casino, nine restaurants, five bars and lounges, 60,000 square feet of meeting facilities and 20,000-square-foot spa, and 2.3 acres of pool area with fire and water features and outdoor entertainment stage will eventually be joined by a shopping mall, condominiums and additional high-rise and low-rise structures.

A: Exterior **B:** *Promenade corridor* **C:** *Lobby stair* **D:** *Registration*
Photography: *Alise O'Brien/Opulence Studios*

The M Resort is complete in its current form, nonetheless. Its open and transparent public areas offer views of the pool area and the Strip from vast expanses of glass in every venue, and a linear flow to circulation that lets guests reach their destinations quickly and easily, unlike many conventional, inward-looking, maze-like Las Vegas interiors. Of course, grand gestures exist too, including a glass ceiling and water feature in the lobby, a 30,000-square-foot section of the casino ceiling covered in mother of pearl, and a shimmering, palm tree-lined Viaggio Del Sole pool. Yet the visual language is powerful in its restraint. Chic, linear modern forms and spaces

are finished in such stylish materials as Diano Reale, Noce Travertine, glass, stainless steel and Italian Black Walnut. They are complemented by architecturally inspired, contemporary Italian furnishings to surround patrons in a refined and elegant environment that recognizes what it's like to live year-round in the non-stop, anything-goes, over-the-top celebration that is Las Vegas today.

A: Lobby   B: Registration desk   C: Casino

Steak and seafood restaurants are typically masculine in tone, celebrating the ritual of male bonding with dark wood cabinetry, robust traditional furnishings, and deep, saturated colors. The new Terzetto Restaurant and Oyster Bar at the M Resort, in Henderson, Nevada, brings a fresh, award-winning vision to the genre. The 11,850-square-foot, 269-seat restaurant, designed by Marnell Architecture, is characterized by clean lines, glowing and suspended architectural elements, contemporary furnishings, warm colors and rich materials that include teak wood, glass walls, Belgium Black Marble, Broccato Marble and suspended glass bubbles. Consequently, the open, elegant and sophisticated interiors of the dining room, full bar, private dining room, large, outdoor dining terrace and chef's table surveying the exhibition cooking line—all enjoying vistas of the pool and Las Vegas Strip—appeals to men and women alike. Terzetto's location is equally calculating. Strategically positioned to the west of the M Resort's registration lobby with its east façade exposed to the gaming floor, it lets diners reach the restaurant without having to cross the gaming floor while remaining readily accessible to the gaming customer. A menu featuring great steak and seafood can inspire hunger at any time, and Terzetto is ready to satisfy it.

A: Private dining room B: Bar C: Dining room D: Suspended dining table
***Photography:** Alise O'Brien/Opulence Studios*

It's no secret that the spa and salon experience is an intensely pleasurable exercise in self-indulgence, now that it has become increasingly popular among both men and women concerned about their health, fitness and personal appearance. Paradoxically, a visit is both public, involving social interaction with fellow patrons, and private, offering opportunities for solo contemplation. The new, 23,000-square-foot Spa & Salon Mio at the M Resort, in Henderson, Nevada, designed by Marnell Architecture, pampers customers by establishing specialized areas that are as much social settings as they are operational facilities, including 16 treatment rooms, fitness facility, full salon with dedicated barber station, common lounges, and men's and women's locker rooms. All areas are sumptuously appointed in fine materials, including Noce Travertine, Venetian Plaster, colored glass, and walnut hardwood and veneer, that are complemented by sleek, contemporary furnishings, a full spectrum of sophisticated lighting, and a color scheme emphasizing warm tones and rich textures, to make every experience memorable. The arrangement should even accommodate growth with minimal strain. By paying careful attention to the placement and adjacencies of mechanical, electrical and plumbing functions, Marnell Architecture's design can facilitate future expansion without interrupting operations, demonstrating a suppleness customers would admire.

A: Entry *B:* Corridor *C:* Salon *D:* Reception
E: Lounge
Photography: Alise O'Brien/Opulence Studios

MARNELL ARCHITECTURE   The M Resort | Marinelli's | Henderson, Nevada

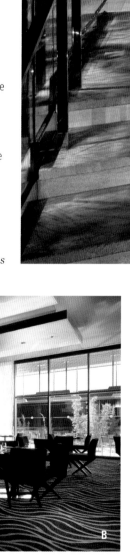

What could be more delightful than an invitation to an Italian family's dining table? Marinelli's Restaurant, a new, 5,337-square-foot, 184-seat restaurant at the M Resort, in Henderson, Nevada, has been designed by Marnell Architecture to create the optimum atmosphere for this privilege. The upscale restaurant, comprising a dining room, full bar, private dining room, exhibition kitchen and wine tasting room, conjures a sense of family familiarity by incorporating the feel of Italy's different regions in a modern architectural environment. To achieve its blend of rustic and urban themes, the design makes inspired use of such materials as Noce Travertine, Grecale Brown Onyx, embedded grass laminated glass, colored glass and rich draperies, contemporary furnishings that are stylish yet informal, a color palette of warm and comforting hues, and an array of direct and indirect lighting. Not only does Marinelli's design perfectly complement its authentic, regional Italian cuisine, it provides diners a unique view of the action in the casino. Raised 12 inches above the gaming floor and enclosed in full-height glass walls, the restaurant can be seen directly off the gaming floor without being disrupted by its sounds. After all, the sounds within Marinelli's should be music enough to customers' ears.

A: Private dining   B: Dining room
C: Entrance and hostess desk   D: Bar
E: Raised dining alcove
***Photography:** Alise O'Brien/Opulence Studios*

Inspired by an old Italian speedboat, the Veloce Cibo restaurant at the M Resort, in Henderson, Nevada, welcomes diners to an elegant and comfortable décor that evokes the vessel's warm wood planks and polished metal accents—plus a spectacular view of the Las Vegas Strip. The new, 9,689-square-foot, 234-seat space, designed by Marnell Architecture, is an upscale restaurant with dining room, bar, private dining room and outdoor dining area that sits atop the M Resort's 16-story guest tower, served by a street-level entrance and separate elevator that avoid distracting hotel guests. To create complete views of the Strip and mountains to the west, the design team located the kitchen along the south side of the tower as part of the careful planning that inserted the fully functional restaurant, bar and kitchen within the tower's footprint. The same attention to detail is also visible in such critical elements as the sleek, contemporary interiors of Santos mahogany, Brazilian cherry, backlit image glass, terra cotta and colored glass, and the chic yet inviting modern furnishings. With diners spreading word of the bar's superb cocktails and the kitchen's imaginative

menu, Veloce Cibo has quickly become a popular destination where the sky's literally the limit.

*A: Bar/lounge **B:** Entrance **C:** Communal dining room **D:** Dining room*
Photography: *Alise O'Brien/Opulence Studios*

Driven by a fresh vision of contemporary architecture that is friendly, elegant and stylish without being ostentatious, the 390 guestrooms at the M Resort, in Henderson, Nevada, have been designed by Marnell Architecture to complement the distinctive image of the resort and casino that deliberately courts the residents of Las Vegas along with out-of-town guests. Emphasizing timeless elegance over trendy ostentation while offering every convenience and comfort visitors expect of Las Vegas resorts, the M Resort's accommodations range from guestrooms and classic one-bedroom suites to end suites and loft suites, all ideally planned to promote rest, relaxation and entertaining. The award-winning design of the hotel's accommodations

is based on a material palette of Diano Reale, Noce Travertine, Italian Black Walnut and Chocolate Marble, furnished with modern furniture that is crisply tailored yet comfortable, and oriented to provide optimum views, with end suites stacked on the east tip of the tower and loft suites stacked on the west tip.

A: View area in loft suite   B: Suite bedroom
C: Suite bathroom   D: Guest accomodations
entrance   E: Loft suite living area
***Photography:** Alise O'Brien/Opulence Studios*

MARNELL ARCHITECTURE

Of course, since guests choose suites for a more luxurious experience than standard guestrooms, classic one-bedroom and flat suites are enhanced by such features as a separate powder room, executive office area, separate living space and conversation bar, while two-story loft suites offer 270-degree views of the Las Vegas skyline along with private entries, two separate living areas featuring stone-and-glass staircases and etched sliding glass doors, multiple HD flat screen LCD televisions and wet bars, and bathrooms that come with freestanding spa tubs and separate steam showers. Direct access from the registration lobby that avoids crossing the paths of gaming patrons, generous individual room proportions, and custom furnishings and décor in rich tones and textures that project a residential feel deliver the finishing touches to make a stay at the M Resort unique, memorable and highly satisfying.

A: Guest bedroom   B: Guest bathroom
C: View of suite showcasing bedroom and living area

MBH Architects

MBH ARCHITECTS Yard House | Red Rock Casino | Las Vegas, Nevada

A: Booths in dining room B: Entry lobby
C: Exterior D: Bar
Photography: *Misha Bruk, Bruk Studios*

The Yard House at the Red Rock Casino, in Las Vegas, projects the kind of irrepressible energy and distinctive character that draws customers for anything from family dining to business cocktails. This 475-seat, 11,066-square-foot restaurant has been designed by MBH Architects as a warm, dark and relaxing environment where over 200 different beers and hearty fare are served with spectacular views of the San Gabriel Mountains. The high-tech contemporary interior features wood, stainless steel, stone, blackened metal and casual furnishings. To accompany such brews as Bayhawk Beach Blonde, Newcastle Brown and Big Sky Moose Drool

and entrées that include Maui chicken, New York steak and pan-seared ahi, the Yard House surrounds its wide-open dining room and central bar with a glass-enclosed keg room, open and elevated kitchen, and 40-seat outdoor patio. Each space is uniquely designed for visual interest as well as utility, along with a connection to the casino. The keg room, for example, proudly displays its kegs, structure and plumbing like a science fiction film's set design, while the kitchen mounts a dazzling spectacle to rival the 27 television screens and state-of-the-art music system. To beer aficionados, the design clearly proclaims: The Yard House is your house.

194

MBH Architects   Café Bistro, Ebar | Nordstrom | Cerritos, California

Nordstrom's customers have two new and delectable reasons to keep shopping at the upscale retailer's Cerritos, California location. The Café Bistro, a 106-seat, 2,930-square-foot restaurant, and the Ebar, an 865-square-foot coffee bar, both designed by MBH Architects, have opened to let shoppers pause for moments or minutes in style, comfort and convenience before returning to the selling floor. The Café is a cozy and inviting space that features an exhibition cookline, a unique color palette of specially chosen finishes, a collection of smart looking yet comfortable furnishings, attractive examples of contemporary art on the walls, and distinctive lighting set off by a series of oversized pendant lamp shades. Besides introducing an attractive milieu for food and conversation, the

restaurant opens a rare and scenic glimpse of the surrounding landscape, which most retail environments understandably ignore. At a much smaller scale, the Ebar creates a convivial setting for coffee and snacks that combines an inviting floor plan, attractive cabinetry for display, service and bar-style food and beverage consumption, and warm lighting characterized by pendant fixtures. Here the emphasis is on ease of use, letting shoppers indulge themselves in a little treat that Nordstrom serves with its usual panache.

*A: Cookline in Café Bistro **B:** Interior of Café Bistro **C:** Interior of Ebar **D:** Café Bistro entrance **E:** Ebar entrance*
***Photography:** Misha Bruk, Bruk Studios*

MBH Architects   Pedro's Cantina | San Francisco, California

Directly across the street from AT&T Park in San Francisco's SoMa (South of Market Street) district, Pedro's Cantina is a sprawling, 474-seat, 8,000-square-foot sports bar that knows its customers and how to please them. The open, bright and festively colored space has been designed by MBH Architects to put sports fans in the center of the action wherever they sit, just steps away from the home of the San Francisco Giants. Starting with the space's high ceiling, the design takes advantage of the building's timber framing by leaving it exposed

to establish a friendly, informal atmosphere that is complemented by a spacious central bar, 100-seat mezzanine, sturdy clusters of table seating where everyone has a clear view of the space, exposed brick walls, and straightforward lighting scheme that does not overshadow the restaurant's high-tech audio/visual system, featuring 24 50-inch flat screen televisions. What gives Pedro's Cantina its robust appeal is its skill in recreating the sense of community that thrives next door, so that sports fans can keep the spirit of the game alive as they

indulge in jalapeño-spiked Pedro's margaritas and other favorite beverages over heaping platters of tacos, burritos, quesadillas, tostaditas, tamales and nachos.

A: Bar and high-stool tables   B: Mezzanine view of bar   C: Exterior at entrance   D: Main floor and mezzanine
Photography: *Misha Bruk, Bruk Studios*

D

MBH Architects   Epic Roasthouse and Waterbar | San Francisco, California

When Rincon Park opened as part of San Francisco's resurgent Embarcadero waterfront, it embraced a novelty: "Cupid's Span," a giant bow and arrow embedded in the northern tip of the park, the work of artists Claes Oldenberg and Coosje Van Bruggen. Two commercial restaurants at the southern end were designed by MBH Architects in collaboration with Engstrom Design Group and restaurateur Pat Kuleto. A special arrangement between developer JMA and the Port of San Francisco allowed Epic Roasthouse and Waterbar to use public land for two enclosed structures totaling 18,000 square feet on either side of a shared 5,600-square-foot outdoor seating plaza. Kuleto envisioned the restaurants to resemble adaptations of Industrial Age buildings, namely a powerhouse for Epic and pump house for Waterbar. Consequently, the architecture employs Industrial Age materials, including brick, limestone and darkened metals, to produce two contemporary icons. Epic is a steakhouse that conjures its powerhouse identity with thin horizontal roofs capping ribbons of windows atop a limestone plinth

and an indoor/outdoor stone fireplace with cylindrical metal chimney, while Waterbar gives Kuleto's fish house a pump house of tall windows between slender brick piers enclosing a two-story dining room with a brick vaulted ceiling.

A: Waterbar and Epic Roasthouse seen against Bay Bridge   *B: Epic Roasthouse entrance*   *C: Rincon restaurants at dusk*
Photography: *Farshid Assassi/Assassi Productions*

Peter Fillat Architects

509 S Exeter Street, Suite 200 • Baltimore, Maryland 21202 • 410.576.9310 • 410.576.8565 (Fax)

www.pfarc.com

PETER FILLAT ARCHITECTS Miramar Courtyard by Marriot | Ocean City, Maryland

It's a big job satisfying eight million vacationers who come each year to Ocean City, a year-round resort on Maryland's Eastern Shore boasting a 10-mile beachfront, three-mile boardwalk and a seemingly infinite number of eateries and shops. Miramar Courtyard by Marriott is a 91-room, four-story, 95,000-square-foot hotel, designed by Peter Fillat Architects, that knows what the public wants. This resort-style Courtyard by Marriott offers such family-oriented facilities as the main lobby/lounge, banquet room, business center, meeting rooms, Captain's Table restaurant (an Ocean City favorite for over 50 years), indoor/outdoor pool with retractable roof, outside sun deck and lounge, on- and off-site parking as well as guestrooms. What gives the hotel its signature look is the design's spirited blend of Art Deco and nautical themes, which are expressed in curvilinear forms, a color palette of white, light greens and blues, and silver against rich wood paneling, such materials as hardwood, stone, ceramic tile, vinyl wallcovering, custom terrazzo flooring, carpet, Art Deco-style furnishings, and architecturally integrated lighting. Miramar Courtyard by Marriott manages to be simultaneously joyous and graceful, pleasing young and old just as Ocean City has been doing for over a century.

A: Outdoor lounge   B: Exterior   C: Business center   D: Main lobby/reception
Photography: *Paul Burk Photography*

A

Bringing a piece of urban sophistication to the suburbs, the new CityStay Hotel prototype is designed to satisfy those travelers who yearn for the coolness factor. This 90-room boutique hotel was recognized at the 2007 Wave of the Future awards program held at the *Hospitality Design* Magazine Boutique Hotel Show. Reminiscent of an urban skyline, the hotel features an open lobby/bar scene and guestrooms with wood floors. A series of reflecting pools are dynamically lit and flow from the lobby to the outside pool garden environment. Designed to be incorporated into mixed-use developments, the room module stacks over garage automobile layouts without transferring structural requirements. Complemented by a menu of popular services, a stylish palette of finishes, and staff dressed in airline-inspired uniforms, CityStay will build a new hospitality brand for the next generation.

A: Exterior   B: Atrium lobby   C: Porte cochere at entrance   D: Guestroom   E: Guest bath F: Lobby lounge/bar
Illustrations: *Courtesy of Peter Fillat Architects*

PETER FILLAT ARCHITECTS   Queenstown Harbor Resort | Queenstown, Maryland

This 4-star eco-boutique style resort is nestled within the 36-hole championship golf course known as Queenstown Harbor. The property will have approximately 120 hotel rooms with 80 rooms in the main building and the additional 40 rooms divided between five two story Golf Villas. Queenstown Harbor Resort will offer a 7,000-square-foot full-service spa, exercise and yoga rooms, and a full-service restaurant and lounge, as well as 6,400-square-feet of meeting space which includes a 4,200-square-foot ballroom, an outdoor pool and lounge, outdoor dining areas, and outdoor gathering spaces and amenities. The facilities will incorporate solar hot water systems, geothermal heating, green roofs, indigenous materials, and rainwater collection and reuse. This project will embrace sustainable design practices and seek LEED Gold certification.

The existing property and golf course present a unique environment for guests to experience. Situated on the Chester River and surrounded by the beauty of the Mid-Atlantic this resort will offer luxurious accommodations amidst the escapism provided by the property's wildlife preserve, nature trails, and waterfront activities. Queenstown Harbor Resort will seek to embody the uniqueness of the place it inhabits in order to create an intimate and memorable guest experience.

A: *Waterside elevation* **B:** *View from Chesapeake Bay* **C:** *Entrance* **D:** *Exterior at putting green*
Illustrations: *Courtesy of Peter Fillat Architects*

The George Washington | A Wyndham Grand Hotel | Winchester, Virginia

While everyone appreciates the historic charm and Old World comfort of a Georgian Revival-style hotel built in 1924 and fully restored with modern services and amenities, structures like the beloved George Washington Hotel, in Winchester, Virginia, are difficult to resurrect. First of all, modern hotel accommodations do not fit readily into older construction like the constricted depth room bays of the 90-room, six-floor, 76,000-square-foot hotel. In addition, the Wyndham's brand standard for its Historic Hotels

typically require the introduction of new functional areas where space for additional construction is often limited. Fortunately, the renovation of the George Washington, designed by Peter Fillat Architects, benefited from the design team's comprehensive knowledge of the hospitality industry, and its eagerness to engage the building's historic and idiosyncratic framework. Not only are the new guestrooms highly desirable in terms of space, function and amenity—while respecting the building's integrity—the new spa/pool and restaurant have been handsomely installed in the underutilized basement. Of course, George Washington discloses nothing to guests about how it developed its splendid, new or remodeled lobby, lounge, ballroom, spa, guestrooms, meeting rooms, restaurant, kitchen, display kitchen, administrative areas and restrooms. Discretion is the trademark of a timeless, classic hotel—and its designer.

*A: Historic exterior B: Restored entrance
C: Restaurant D: Ballroom E: Bar F: Lobby
Photography: Paul Burk Photography*

RANDY BURKETT LIGHTING DESIGN

RANDY BURKETT LIGHTING DESIGN   Four Seasons Hotel | St. Louis, Missouri

The opening of the 200-room Four Seasons St. Louis, featuring interior design by BraytonHughes and lighting design by Randy Burkett Lighting Design, records an intriguing milestone for Laclede's Landing, a 19th-century St. Louis riverfront neighborhood and vibrant entertainment district beside the iconic Gateway Arch. Considered the most elegant new hotel in a city where numerous distinguished hotels occupy historic buildings, the Four Seasons is part of Lumière Place, a development that adds a second casino to "The Landing." The hotel's design reflects its proximity to the casino as well as its own world-class standards. Consequently, custom-designed lighting in special event spaces reinforces an overall strategy to differentiate the Four Seasons from competing properties. Ballroom chandeliers woven from extruded polymer fibers and tipped with glass beads glow with light from end-fiber illuminators in the ceiling, choreographed by a central dimming system that can shift effortlessly from elegant white light displays to color settings or sequences. Lobbies and other public spaces are also uniquely illuminated, employing such techniques as recessed adjustable accent lighting and architecturally concealed detail illumination. Even the spa receives close attention, with overhead LED light planes letting clients select their own reinforcing color experience or a soothing pre-programmed one.

A: Guest suite   B: Lobby   C: Ballroom
Photography: *Debbie Franke Photography, Inc.*

RANDY BURKETT LIGHTING DESIGN Lumière Place Casino | St. Louis, Missouri

Paddlewheelers departing for dinner cruises or sightseeing from Laclede's Landing on the Mississippi River in downtown St. Louis are picturesque reminders of the commercial life that once thrived in this historic neighborhood of cobblestone streets and 19th-century warehouses. Today, The Landing flourishes as an entertainment district, thanks to such developments as Lumière Place, where the new, 75,000-square-foot Lumière Place Casino and renovated, 294-room HoteLumière St. Louis were designed by a project team including HOK, Marnell Architects and Randy Burkett Lighting Design. Lighting for the casino and hotel is vital in creating

a stimulating, nighttime presence for the gaming environment, and simultaneously maintains a refined decorum for another major component of the development, the Four Seasons hotel. To establish equilibrium between gaming and lodging, the lighting in Lumière's restaurants and other amenity spaces emphasizes their clean, uncomplicated architectural lines and casual, low-key ambiance to signal a departure from dynamic gaming areas. Transition areas throughout the building are likewise illuminated, combining high efficiency linear sources with halogen-based accenting lighting to promote a seamless, property-wide experience. In these and

various other ways, lighting has been indispensable to Lumière's success from the start, giving The Landing a new destination as memorable as itself.

A: Casino entrance   B: Cocktail lounge
C: Restaurant bar   D: Community table in restaurant
Photography: *Alise O'Brien Photography, Debbie Franke Photography, Inc.*

Judy Garland and the cast of the classic 1944 movie, Meet Me in St. Louis, would feel at home at the new, 90,000-square-foot River City Casino, occupying the former National Paint Co. factory in St. Louis. That's because the renovation, designed by Bergman, Walls and Associates, architect, Avery Brooks and Associates, interior designer, and Randy Burkett Lighting Design, lighting designer, incorporates Garland's fictional family home as a steakhouse, one of numerous restaurants, bars, shops and a cocktail lounge that serve casino patrons. What's more, owner Pinnacle Entertainment worked closely with the design team to capture the look and feel of the Mississippi riverfront during the peak of the steamboat era, consulting old photographs to recreate elements of the 1904 St. Louis Exposition, to satisfy project requirements from the Missouri Gaming Commission. Lighting is critical to the spacious, ornate and highly detailed environment. To support River City's storyline, the thematic scheme draws on efficient metal halide, LED and fluorescent sources, adding halogen in key applications, for both functional and aesthetic illumination. Not only does River City revive the sense of wonder visitors experienced at the fair over 100 years ago, it employs 21st-century techniques that never intrude on the fun.

*A: Judy's Velvet Lounge at River City **B:** The Beerhouse at River City **C:** 1940 Steakhouse at River City **D:** Casino*
Photography: *Debbie Franke Photography, Inc.*

A

Against all odds, a landmark hotel that defined excellence in St. Louis in 1917 as the Statler Hotel has triumphantly emerged from years in limbo as the Renaissance Grand Hotel. The restoration and expansion, designed by RTKL, architect, ForrestPerkins, interior designer, and Randy Burkett Lighting Design, lighting designer, not only provides modern luxury accommodations, including the original, 275-room hotel, a new, 600-room tower and a new, 55,000-square-foot ballroom and meeting facility atop an adjacent parking structure. It also returns the lobby, atrium and 22nd-floor ballroom to their original appearance. Balancing historic precedence with contemporary need, the lighting design helps integrate old and new spaces. For example, to showcase the original hotel lobby as the new premier dining

facility, historically accurate pendant lighting fixtures (based on period photographs) were installed and supplemented with carefully integrated accent lights. Dramatic lighting embellishes the original atrium as the staging area for the hotel's three-meal restaurant. An expansive chandelier whose intricate glass structure comes with its own catwalk for ease of maintenance anchors the new adjacent lobby space. Lighting even rejuvenates the historic façade, thanks to recreated sconces holding high-efficiency lamps and metal halide luminaires concealed in the original cornice.

A: *Original ballroom* **B:** *Lounge* **C:** *Exterior*
D: *Lobby mezzanine*
Photography: *Alise O'Brien Photography*

RANDY BURKETT LIGHTING DESIGN   American Queen Riverboat | New Orleans, Louisiana

Mark Twain never plied the Mississippi onboard the American Queen—and that's the honest truth. Modeled to resemble the legendary riverboats of the 19th century, the American Queen is a modern vessel built by the McDermott shipyard with environmental design by Communication Arts, for the Delta Queen Steamboat Company to take vacationers on cruises along the Mississippi and Ohio Rivers. Its design represents a calculated blend of picturesque imagery and modern technology, so it incorporates such features as two extra propellers that can handle situations where its relatively small paddle wheels prove insufficient. While its 418-foot length, 89-foot, 4-inch height, and 222 staterooms for up to 436 passengers make it one of the largest riverboats ever constructed, the Queen discreetly clothes its state-of-the-art facilities in period dress. That's why the lighting design by Randy Burkett Lighting Design is devoted to capturing the look

and feel of the Victorian age whether or not the lighting fixtures are on display. This means 21st-century sources are masked or concealed from view to let period-style ornamental luminaires parade their atmospheric charm. Right down to the carbon-filament lamps that are proudly incorporated in its lovingly assembled décor, the American Queen tells a tale as entertaining as *Tom Sawyer.*

A: Dining room   B: Theater   C: Exterior
D: Grand staircase
Photography: *Delta Queen Steamboat Company*

Fine dining in shopping malls has evolved from an oxymoron to an option as America's taste for sophisticated fare grows. Yet guests entering Wapango, a Pan-Latin restaurant at the Chesterfield Mall, in Chesterfield, Missouri, still find themselves enthralled even before they take their seats by the bold, contemporary space designed by Tao + Lee, architect, and Randy Burkett Lighting Design, lighting designer. Naturally, inspiration for the design (huapango is a Mexican folk dance) comes from the Mexican, Central and South American cultures that inform its

cuisine. The brick façade is enriched with copper panels set into illuminated niches that are visible from the highway. Inside, the dining room, bar, elevated party level and private dining room form interlocking zones that trace a graceful arc. Lighting supplies the finishing touches indoors and out. While individual tables and booths are illuminated by recessed adjustable downlights, themed decorative luminaries reinforce color and vibrancy, concealed linear and low-voltage sources detail millwork and architectural forms, and accent lights highlight

artwork and featured finishes. Equally important, the lighting that intensifies a color palette of papaya, mango, turquoise and red also provides complements such imaginative entrées as adobo-seasoned chicken, Yucatan tacos and crab-spinach enchiladas.

A: Exterior B: Party level C: Dining room
Photography: *Fentress Photography*

RDH Interest's Inc.

RDH Interest's inc   Aria Spa and Salon | Aria | Las Vegas, Nevada

A

Everything about CityCenter, an 18 million-square-foot, mixed-use development on 67 acres lining the Strip in Las Vegas, has been larger than life, including its roster of eight leading international architects working in a design collaboration with MGM Resorts International. Thus, the new, 70,000-square-foot Aria Spa and Salon at CityCenter's 4,004-room Aria Resort & Casino, designed by RDH Interest's as interior designer of record, Super Potato from Japan as conceptual designer, and F&M Architecture Inc. as architect of record, represented a prestigious and highly visible facility that was expected to meet the highest standards of design to succeed. Not only has the design achieved LEED certification for

its embrace of green design, it has faithfully created the cutting-edge look and use of materials called for by Super Potato—making it immediately popular with the affluent, sophisticated and fashion-forward customers now flocking to its lobby, salon, gym, changing rooms, nail rooms, massage rooms and circulation spaces. Importantly, the airy and elegantly austere contemporary interior, constructed largely of natural stone, wood and glass and outfitted with stylish, minimalist furnishings and sophisticated lighting, represents an oasis of serenity and tranquility that even the liveliest and most indefatigable visitors to Las Vegas can appreciate.

A: Pool in gym   B: Massage room   C: Salon
Photography: *Provided by MGM Resorts International*

B

C

RDH Interest's inc   Jean Philippe Pâtisserie | Bellagio | Las Vegas, Nevada

For the Bellagio, the 3,933-room luxury resort and casino that ushered in the post-Vegas-is-for-families era of refined elegance in 1998, the addition of the Spa Tower has brought more than 928 new rooms and suites. Along with 60,000 square feet of meeting and convention space, an expanded spa, new retail outlets, and Sensi restaurant, Bellagio now has Jean Philippe Pâtisserie, a chic, 1,200-square-foot, European-style pastry shop with its own entry in the Guinness Book of World Records. Designed by RDH Interest's as interior designer of record and NODA as conceptual designer, Jean Philippe Pâtisserie is a dazzling contemporary retail environment that treats its elegant pastries and chocolates as precious objects to be admired for their form as well as enjoyed for their flavor, texture and aroma. The design lives up to its role, surrounding the confections in a boutique-like ambiance of cool Japanese white glass walls, a warm copper floor overlaid by glass, and a suspended glass sculpture that is highlighted by dramatic lighting along with the food. Why the Guinness citation? It's for the world's largest chocolate fountain. To everyone's credit, the fountain is just one of many visual delights in a space good enough to eat.

A: Storefront
Photography: *Randall D. Huggins*

A

People may increasingly tell time by consulting cell phones, tablet computers or music players, but watches persist in the digital era—as jewelry if not timepieces. If fact, today's watches are dazzling fashion accessories that accent wardrobes and social settings, and that is exactly how the Watch Shop, designed by RDH Interest's as architect of record and interior designer of record, treats its merchandise at Treasure Island, in Las Vegas. Sleek contemporary display cases accented by traditional table lamps await shoppers beneath coffered ceilings and dramatic lighting, sparkling like jewel-encrusted islands on a selling floor framed by light-washed walls with built-in vitrines. If the neatly tailored, 2,100-square-foot showroom of wood, glass, lacquer, wallcovering and carpet looks emphatically adult in what was once known as a kid-friendly pirate paradise, it's because Treasure Island, now known simply as TI, has grown up. Not only has the famed skull-and-crossbones marquee been replaced by a sleek design bearing the initials TI, the long-running outdoor "Buccaneer Bay" show of pirates raiding a coastal village has given way to "The Sirens of TI," a steamy performance where sexy sirens tame bare-chested pirates—hopefully with the entire cast sporting superb timepieces from The Watch Shop.

A: Storefront B: Showroom
Photography: *Randall D. Huggins*

Named one of the top 100 hotels in the United States and Canada by *Travel + Leisure* magazine, the 1,740-room Beau Rivage Resort & Casino opened on the Gulf Coast in Biloxi, Mississippi in 1999 and reopened after a dramatic, post-Katrina, $550-million renovation in 2006. Praised for its original facilities, Beau Rivage raised the stakes with architecture and interior design that gave the resort's signature Southern charm and elegance a contemporary edge, reconfigured the casino floor to upgrade and expand gaming areas, created a spectacular new image for the atrium and lobby, and refreshed and modernized the spa, salon and guest rooms. Among the new retail shops contributing to the renaissance of the resort is a 2,500-square-foot store for The Watch Shop, designed by RDH Interest's as architect of record and interior designer of record. The stately Neoclassical interior, consisting of finely detailed wood millwork and trim, stylish wallcoverings, richly patterned carpet, and period-style lighting fixtures, is thoroughly infused with the ambiance of the new Beau Rivage. Equally impressive is the store's seemingly effortless ability to handle very tight space requirements. The power of design, besides revitalizing Beau Rivage, has worked its magic in The Watch Shop as well.

A: Storefront   B: Showroom
Photography: *Randall D. Huggins*

Even passionate casino players enjoy a break from the action to relax and refocus, and those gaming at the 1,740-room Beau Rivage Resort & Casino, in Biloxi, Mississippi, have a delectable getaway, the 875 Lounge, awaiting them right off the casino. Of course, Beau Rivage's 85,000-square-foot casino delivers plenty of excitement, thanks to 93 table games, 2,100 slot machines, 230 video poker games, a two-tiered, 16-table poker room, and a luxurious high-roller area. Yet the 95-seat, 2,200-square-foot lounge and service bar, designed by RDH Interest's as architect of record and interior designer of record to occupy a space that originally housed a retail store, offers seductive charms of its own. The traditional interior projects a contemporary edge, an intimate space that is stylishly appointed in leather and wood wallcoverings, wood veneered ceiling, laminated glass in the bar and bar ceiling, carpet, transitional furnishings, a lighting scheme featuring a half mile of neon in and above the bar, and a sound system that erects a wall of music around the space without overflowing to the casino. Not only do guests like the 875 Lounge, *Restaurant and Lounge* cited it as one of the Top 100 Lounges of 2005.

A: *Bar* **B:** *Table for four* **C:** *Lounge seating area* **D:** *Banquette seating*
Photography: *Ron Calamia*

Shopping is one of the key pleasures of any vacation, and guests of the Beau Rivage Resort & Casino, in Biloxi, Mississippi, have many choices to sample in the skillfully reconfigured and handsomely refurbished retail promenade that is part of the Beau Rivage's triumphant rebirth following Hurricane Katrina. Da Milano draws attention to its designer shoes and accessories by displaying them in a luxurious, traditional, 2,600-square-foot interior, designed by RDH Interest's as architect of record and interior designer of record, that establishes an ambiance of style and comfort despite very tight space requirements. Using wallcovering, wood, carpet and a modular, circular-shaped ceiling system to create the feeling of an elegant salon, sophisticated lighting that bathes everything in a soft, warm glow, a custom-designed wood millwork display system that can be modified to suit the merchandise being shown, and traditional furnishings that could easily grace a prestigious private residence, Da Milano turns shopping into a glamorous and memorable experience. It's one more reason why Beau Rivage thrives as the largest resort in the Southeast to receive the AAA Four Diamond award, recognized by both *Conde Nast Traveler* and *Travel + Leisure* as one of the top resorts in the country.

A: Showroom   B: Storefront
Photography: *Randall D. Huggins*

Want more than gaming, entertainment, shopping and fine dining? For the last two decades, Las Vegas has enlisted fine art as yet another potent draw in making itself one of the world's top destinations. So the arrival of a survey of current work by world-renowned glass sculptor Dale Chihuly represents a win-win-win for visitors, artist and community. The venue could not be more appropriate. The Gallery is a 4,350-square-foot exhibition space within Crystals, a 500,000-square-foot retail component of CityCenter, a prestigious, 67-acre, 18-million-square-foot, mixed-use development on the Strip, designed by an ensemble of distinguished architects—Crystals is credited to Daniel Libeskind and David Rockwell—for a joint venture between MGM Resorts International and Dubai's Infinity World Development. The Dale Chihuly Gallery was designed by RDH Interest's as architect of record and interior designer of record to carry out the conceptual design by Chihuly himself. What distinguishes the dramatic, four-showroom space, a LEED-certified project, is the understated yet supportive role of contemporary architecture in presenting Chihuly's famed glass pieces, using basic rectilinear form, neutral color, good circulation flow, brilliant lighting and unobtrusive structural support for each work of art, giving visitors an encounter with Chihuly's vision they will never forget.

A: Display employing cantilevered shelves
B: Suspended and elevated supporting structures
C: Wall mounted painting and freestanding
pedestal D: Grid of cube-like vitrines
E: Display of mixed media
Photography: *Randall D. Huggins*

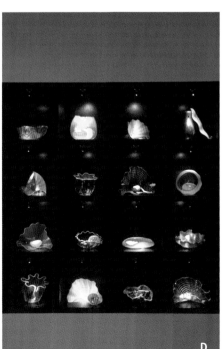

RESORT INTERIORS

As one of America's premier family and beach vacation destinations, Myrtle Beach, South Carolina attracts 14 million visitors annually who come to enjoy the beautiful beaches and plentiful golf courses. The opening of the new Anderson Ocean Club and Spa, a sumptuous, 496-room hotel and condominium featuring Addison Mizner-inspired Mediterranean Revival architecture and interior design by Resort Interiors, illustrates what families want. Guestrooms, ranging from studios to 3-bedroom units, spa, pool and fitness center cater to families, groups, golfers, couples and business travelers with facilities that are "formal without being stuffy." Attractive, comfortable yet durable to withstand the busy summers and ocean environment, the design boasts a rich color palette, custom casegoods with serpentine-shaped fronts and select hardwoods, and custom fabric and carpet bearing the architecture's decorative motifs. Thomas P. Jenkins, project manager of the developer, Strand Capital Group, observes, "As timing is critical with every project, owners never want to hear that someone 'dropped the ball.'

Working with Resort Interiors was one of our best games ever. We tossed them our expectations and they delivered."

A: Entry courtyard B: Guest bedroom C: Guest living room D: Main lobby and registration **Photography:** *Matt Silk*

When the only hotel on the waterfront in historic Hampton, Virginia—a city founded in 1610 whose neighbors include Norfolk Naval Base, Langley Air Force Base, NASA Langley Research Center, and the Virginia Air & Space Center—conducted a multi-million-dollar conversion, embracing a contemporary nautical theme for its new interiors was an inspired decision. The transformation of the former Hampton Radisson into the Crowne Plaza Hampton Marina, designed by Resort Interiors, has produced engaging new environments for the 173 guestrooms and suites and such key public areas as the lobby, ballroom, Latitude 37 lounge and Regatta Grille restaurant. A nautical palette of blues and golds complements the use of polished chrome, teak wood and boating hardware to establish a signature look throughout the property. In one much appreciated makeover, a 1980s-era elevated seating area has reemerged as an elegant "yacht deck"

complete with cable railing, teak and holly deck and seaworthy lounge seating. "The business, military, government and educational community are in awe of the wonderful upgrade," notes Jim Moyler, project manager for the client, MHI Hospitality. "Resort Interiors brought this project in under budget and on time. They are now a part of our team we cannot afford to be without."

A: Guest casegoods   B: Guest bathroom
C: Guestroom beds and bed linens   D: Bay window in guestroom   E: Cable railing detail in lobby   F: Lobby's elevated seating area
Photography: *Matt Silk*

F

Favored for over 40 years by families and couples vacationing in Myrtle Beach, South Carolina, the Caribbean Resort & Villas has completed a $10-million renovation and expansion, featuring interior design by Resort Interiors, that surrounds guests in a gracious and more luxurious milieu with new housing options. New interiors enhance the Dominican Tower, an oceanfront tower of two-room suites, and the newly constructed Cayman Tower, a 20-story structure housing 2-, 3- and 4-bedroom oceanfront condominiums along with the resort's lobbies, lounges, meeting rooms, corridors and amenity spaces. Resort Interiors' design scheme, which can be described as "Old Key West Meets South Carolina Lowcountry," combines a color palette highlighted by soft greens and robin's egg blue with such distinctive materials as grass cloth, pecky cypress and tigerwood, and fine furnishings and accessories. In his comments on how well the renovation and expansion have been received, David L. Brittain, Brittain Resort Management, says, "I would not hesitate to recommend Resort Interiors for any size undertaking."

A: Custom chandelier B: Living room in guest suite C: Main lobby, Cayman Tower
Photography: *Matt Silk*

No one hurries on Pawleys Island, South Carolina, located 70 miles north of Charleston and 25 miles south of Myrtle Beach, which suits guests at The Lodge at Pawleys Island just fine. Pawleys Island, one of the East Coast's oldest summer resorts with only 200 year-round residents but thousands of part-time residents and visitors, began as an 18th-century summer getaway for the families of mainland rice planters, and has honored that vision ever since. Accordingly, The Lodge at Pawleys Island, a new, 120-room hotel designed by Graham Group Architecture with interior design by Resort Interiors,

employs a contemporary take on the Arts & Crafts style to connect guests to the island's family-oriented lifestyle of golf, fishing, biking and boating. The interiors also work in less visible ways. Besides complementing the Lodge's architecture, they use custom, period-style furnishings and millwork, commissioned photography of nearby Brookgreen Gardens, and color palette of sage green, clay, bronze and gold to maximize the function and efficiency of limited space. Their effectiveness prompted David Graham, AIA, of Graham Group Architecture, to declare, "This has been another

successful working relationship with Resort Interiors, and I am sure we will continue working with them in the future."

A: Guest breakfast bar   B: Guest living room
C: Guest bedroom
Photography: *Matt Silk*

ROBERT SINGER & ASSOCIATES, INC.

655 East Valley Road Suite 200 • Basalt, CO 81621 • 970.963.5692

www.robertsingerlighting.com

ROBERT SINGER & ASSOCIATES, INC.   Dusk Nightclub at Caesar's | Caesar's Palace | Atlantic City, New Jersey

Why are seekers of the next big thing lining up at Dusk Nightclub at Caesar's in Caesars Atlantic City? This innovative, 10,000-square-foot space, designed by I Crave Design and SOSH Architect with Robert Singer & Associates as lighting designer, offers a multi-layered, multi-media entertainment venue for 800 people where the two dance floors, DJ booth, three bars, lounges and restrooms are defined by light and sound as much as architecture. Equipped with a state-of-the-art audio/visual system and theatrical lighting, Dusk promotes an ever-changing atmosphere where guests are simultaneously participants and spectators. Not only is the upper level's spacious dance floor served by two bars where guests can survey the action, it is encircled by a VIP seating area overlooking the dance floor. In addition, a secondary dance floor called Dawn on the lower level leads to a lounge boasting scenic ocean views. The installation is a lighting showcase. In the VIP seating area, for example, color-changing LEDs capable of playing low-resolution video create a privileged zone of intimacy. Overall, dynamic color shifting lets the nightclub orchestrate the mood by applying warm colors to architectural details and cool colors to focal areas, setting the scene for explosive music—or a low-key, private event.

A: Dance floor and DJ booth   B: Bar
C: VIP seating area   D: Stair to Dawn
E: Women's room   F: Men's room
Photography: *Eric Millstein, Stephen Leiberman*

To make waves in New York's hip East Village neighborhood, Kurve Restaurant has packaged its pan-Asian bistro menu inside a kaleidoscopic, undulating, non-stop space, designed by Karim Rashid with Robert Singer & Associates as lighting designer. The graceful, sensuous environment, enclosed by floor-to-ceiling glass at a corner location on busy Second Avenue, is a dramatic departure from the Big Apple's relentlessly orthogonal grid. Drawing on his distinctive design vocabulary, Rashid immerses guests in a world of ovaloid-shaped windows, white glass communal table, ceiling-to-floor amorphous bar, sinuous walls and booths, angular, high-gloss white poly chairs, soft organic white lounge chairs, curve patterned floors, and a cut-out window over the restaurant's DJ booth. The lighting design has been conceived

as a faithful accompaniment to this sculptural tour de force. Downlights, uplights and LEDs highlight the curving surfaces and wash the interior and guests in a soft glow that gives them the luster of precious jewels in a display window. Adding further to the unique ambiance, the lighting satisfies the restaurant's desire for color changing capability, the better to capture the mood of the night and create the ideal backdrop for foie gras shumai or Thai-style papaya salad with big-eye tuna.

A: Exterior ***B:*** *Ovaloid-shaped windows*
C: *Entry* ***D:*** *Bar*
Photography: *Karim Rashid*

Robert Singer & Associates, Inc.   Vessel Nightclub | San Francisco, California

A magnificent exposed brick wall that survived both of San Francisco's major 20th century earthquakes anchors Vessel Nightclub, a memorable, subterranean space located close to Union Square beneath retail stores for Giorgio Armani and Niketown. The masonry may be the only immobile object in the 4,500-square-foot space designed by Stephane Dupoux of Dupoux Designs with Robert Singer & Associates as lighting designer. Hosting events ranging from high-energy dancing and relaxed lounging to corporate gatherings, the upscale space contrasts the basement's raw architecture with a sleek interior of modern lounge furnishings, trendy faux fur, Ultrasuede and wood finishes, state-of-the-art light and sound systems and a live juniper tree. Its versatile floor plan accommodates 400 people and provides open areas for seating and dancing, a 40-foot, five-well bar, banquette seating for 150, VIP nooks, stage platform, prep kitchen, ventilated smoking room and unisex bathrooms. Its lighting is equally capable, combining architectural fixtures with color-changing LEDs to transform the space through changes in lighting intensity and color. Custom lighting details such as the backlit bar face and underlit bottle wells are also at home here with novelties such as teak and stainless steel tables offering built-in Champagne buckets and tabletops for dancing.

A: Bar   *B: Banquette seating*   *C: Lounge*
D: Main dance floor and juniper tree
Photography: *Nick Tininenko Photography*

Robert Singer & Associates, Inc.   Stay Hotel | New York, New York

Times Square, New York's fabled Theater District and "Crossroads of the World," blazes to life nightly in a dazzling show of lighting for advertising and architecture. One of its newest spectacles is the Stay Hotel, a chic, 208-room boutique hotel that prides itself on being as stylish outside as its Murano glass chandelier, 18,000-gallon aquarium, and compact, slate-and-burnt-orange guestrooms with 42-inch plasma screens and L'Occitane amenities make it inside. Of course, Stay's façade signage and courtyard display, designed by Robert Singer &

Associates, is as conspicuous as it is stylish to compete with surrounding displays. The award-winning scheme simultaneously projects high-definition images over a four-story banner at the front of the hotel and splashes 10 stories of seamless images across the courtyard. Among its key components are 17 computer-controlled projectors that custom-designed enclosures protect from the elements while allowing maximum heat dissipation, a color-changing search light at the base of the courtyard that generates a beam of light visible for miles, and custom content

that blends seasonal and time-specific images with hotel branding. Interestingly, inclement weather works as well for the lighting as starry nights, causing the projectors' light beams to be visible and reaffirming a Times Square tradition.

A-F: High-definition images projected on the façade
Photography: *Christian Dinh/SPACE 404, Robert Singer*

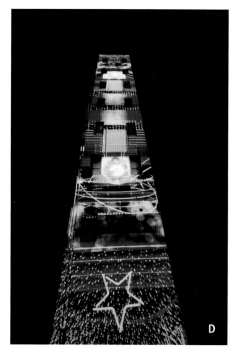

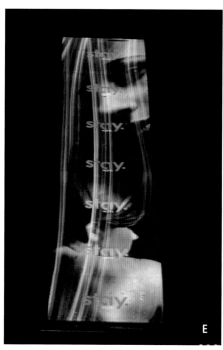

ROBERT SINGER & ASSOCIATES, INC.   President Hotel | New York, New York

America's presidents are the unconventional inspiration for a successful, $15-million renovation that has produced the new, 334-room Best Western President Hotel in Times Square, the heart of New York's Theater District. Thanks to the makeover, designed by Stonehill & Taylor Architects with Robert Singer & Associates as lighting designer, value-conscious guests enjoy stylish guestrooms with modern, eclectic furnishings, upgraded bedding, widescreen TVs, free Wi-Fi and iPod docking stations, along with a chic reception area and lobby,

two restaurants, cocktail bar, state-of-the-art business center and fitness facilities. A sophisticated and programmable lighting design with a "Red, White and Blue" theme provides scenery changes for the façade and interiors throughout the day. The lobby, for example, evolves from a bright, vibrant setting by day to an intimate, romantic one at night. Color-changing LEDs lining curtained walls promote the presidential theme or celebrate a specific holiday. Concealed fixtures in a recessed slot seamlessly graze mosaic tiles along the entrance

hall. Custom shades surround structural columns to turn them into oversized floor lamps. Interior details like these, matched by adjustable fixtures positioned in plants and uplights outside, demonstrate the magic of art and design even when guests aren't sitting down for a Broadway show.

A: Counter in cocktail bar   B: Table seating in cocktail bar   C: Private booth in cocktail bar D: Cocktail bar perspective
Photography: *Gregory Goode*

ROBERT SINGER & ASSOCIATES, INC.   Buddha Bar | New York, New York

Restaurateurs anxious for Zagat and Michelin ratings know that fine dining is a visual experience as well as a culinary one. However, Buddha Bar, in New York's Meat Packing District, blends food and design so seamlessly that guests may not realize how much the décor contributes. Designed by Dupoux Design with Robert Singer & Associates as lighting designer, Buddha Bar provides an eclectic, Asian-inspired environment where the award-winning lighting works closely with the architecture to complement the cuisine. The drama begins in the entry corridor, where uplights flank the gold Buddha statues lining the cylindrical hallway, and continues into the main dining room, where linear lighting frames the ceiling structure and skylight, LED lighting beneath the large Buddha makes the statue "float," and framing projectors and filters create defined patterns of light. Lighting defines other areas with similar precision. At the bar, architectural details incorporate linear LED fixtures to accent bar

faces, backlight bar bottles and float banquettes. The koi ponds below floating private dining pods are illuminated by submersible LEDs. Aquariums with jellyfish behind the bar use a color-changing backdrop to present a stunning tableaux. Is Buddha Bar's appeal based on décor or cuisine? Fortunately, guests can have both.

A: Main dining room   B: Entry corridor
C and D: Bar
Photography: *Christian Dinh*

Stonehill & Taylor Architects, P.C.

31 West 27th Street, Floor 5 • New York, NY 10001 • 212.226.8898 • 212.941.1874 (Fax)

www.stonehilltaylor.com

STONEHILL & TAYLOR ARCHITECTS, P.C. Best Western President Hotel | New York, New York

Guests of the 347 room President Hotel, in New York's legendary theater district, Times Square, are delighted to find showtime begins even before they register. A recent, 115,683 square-foot renovation, designed by Stonehill & Taylor Architects, has rethought, rebranded and redesigned the existing property owned by Hampshire Hotels & Resorts and operated by Best Western. Taking a cue from the property's name, the architect developed a lighthearted visual interpretation of the origins and status of America's presidency and two-party political system that has revitalized the façade, lobby, bar/lounge and guest accommodations, including a fitness center, conference and business

rooms, corridors, guestrooms and suites. Furthermore, the award-winning design incorporates luxury level accoutrements usually found only in European Best Western Premier properties, including featherbeds, Tensel bedding, wool guestroom carpet, plasma TVs and halogen lighting—to raise the guest experience and encourage repeat business. The difference is immediately visible in the once tight and fragmented lobby and other public areas, which have become an open, flexible and welcoming space. Brendan McNamara, vice president of brand development and communications for Hampshire, praised the design, noting, "We always strive to develop the most compelling concepts in our hotels,

and we believe the President Hotel's innovative, relevant design is truly one-of-a-kind."

A: *Lobby*   **B:** *Suite vignette*   **C:** *Obama Suite*
D: *Suite living room*   **E:** *Cocktail bar "Primary"*
F: *Façade*
Photography: *Peter Peirce, Gregory Goode*

STONEHILL & TAYLOR ARCHITECTS, P.C. Crosby Street Hotel | New York, New York

A quiet, cobbled street in New York's vibrant SoHo has become the perfect place to experience the historic neighborhood's bohemian charm and world class shopping, thanks to the arrival of the 86-room Crosby Street Hotel. Designed by Stonehill & Taylor Architects as the first hotel outside of London for the premier luxury London hotelier, Firmdale Hotels, the 11-story, 85,000 square-foot flagship hotel offers bedrooms and suites individually designed and generously proportioned to evoke the quintessential SoHo loft, along with such signature Firmdale amenities as a 99-seat screening room, lounge, meeting rooms, guest library, drawing rooms, and lobby bar and restaurant. Its neighborhood friendly, brick-and-limestone-clad façade, industrial-type windows, and 27-foot setback from the street honor the area's vernacular architecture and evoke the style of SoHo, New York, and the spirit of Firmdale's SoHo hotel property in London.

Unassuming as it appears, the Crosby Street Hotel boasts numerous distinctive features, including original art integrated into the architecture and interiors, such as a gate and bicycle rack by renowned blacksmith James Garvey, memorable, one-of-a-kind furnishings, ranging from a Swedish sofa to a side chair upholstered in Peruvian blankets, and a comprehensive brownfield site remediation program that qualified the hotel to be one of the first LEED Gold certified hotels in New York. Interior Design by Kit Kemp.

*A: Lobby bar and restaurant B: Screening room C: Entrance D: Guestroom E: Suite living room F: Lobby with view of fireplace lounge **Photography:** Simon Brown*

D

E

F

Stonehill & Taylor Architects, P.C. Hyatt Regency New Brunswick | New Brunswick, New Jersey

Attracting business travelers working with Johnson & Johnson and other local companies in New Brunswick, New Jersey, as well as visitors to Rutgers University, nearby historic towns, and New York City, the 288-room Hyatt Regency New Brunswick successfully repositions the existing facility to attain standards on par with Grand Hyatt. The all-inclusive, 51,000 square-foot renovation, designed by Stonehill & Taylor Architects, offers such remodeled and new facilities as the lobby, grand ballroom, meeting spaces, conference center, bar and restaurant, suites, guestroom bathrooms and fitness center, along with new landscaping. Highlights of the award-winning design include the lobby, zoned for a welcome reception; lobby lounge and atrium events space to optimize circulation, bring the outside in, and introduce expressions of nature; the grand hall, featuring a forest image employing wood veneered walls, an overhead canopy of leaves rendered in glass pendants, and a sculpture garden representing a grove of trees; and the lobby lounge, an elegant space appointed in wood planking, fine contemporary furnishings, and artwork featuring panoramic murals of the Raritan River in the 1880s. This design sets the standards for Hyatt conference and meeting centers worldwide.

A: Restaurant B: Grand ballroom
C: Billiards in Restaurant D: Conference room E: Atrium events space F: Lobby lounge
Photography: *Chris Tagart, Peter Peirce*

Because, as lyricists Betty Comden and Adolph Green explained in Leonard Bernstein's immortal "New York, New York," "The Bronx is up and the Battery's down," travelers appreciate midtown Manhattan's Hilton New York for its unparalleled accessibility. The hotel is in the process of completely renovating its 2,000 guestrooms and suites. The new design, by Stonehill & Taylor Architects, renews its identity with the city and makes guestrooms more spacious without moving walls. Inspired by nearby Rockefeller Center's Art Deco architecture, midtown Modernist icons such as the Seagram Building and Lever House, and industrial designer Donald Deskey's brilliant interiors, the design team captured previously underutilized space; created a skyline-based color scheme of blues, whites, creams, and steel gray; installed new furnishings featuring stainless steel hardware, ebonized walnut, luxurious

upholstery and integrated lighting; and introduced a unique architectural element dubbed "the wrapper" to segment guestrooms into three distinct areas. Notes Larry Traxler, Hilton Worldwide's senior vice president of global design services, "Stonehill & Taylor brought in a story line that grounded the design to New York, to the history of the building, and gave it context and background, which was much more interesting than what we typically see in a renovation project."

A: Suite living room   B: Suite study   C: King bedroom   D: Bathroom
Photography: Gregory Goode, Peter Margonelli

WATG

Travelers seeking an authentic connection to the wine culture of California's fabled Napa Valley are delighted to discover a unique lodging named Bardessono. Constructed on a 4.9-acre site at the Bardessono family farmstead, established in 1928 in Yountville in the heart of the Valley, Bardessono is a new, 62-room contemporary luxury hotel, restaurant and spa that is closely linked to the region's architecture and natural environment as well as its wine culture. Developer/owner Philip Sherburne wanted Bardessono to feel personal, warm and genuine, and commissioned WATG to design the architecture in collaboration with Bardessono family descendants, Yountville community representatives, and local craftsmen as well as the project team. The resulting Zen-like, one- and two-story structures not only form a charming, village-like ensemble that gracefully blends with the Valley's architectural vernacular, they include a wide array of environmentally progressive features in their design and operation. Besides embracing such innovations as rooftop solar energy panels, a high-end organic focus in its restaurant, geothermal heating and cooling systems, low-water-flow bathroom fixtures, organic bedding, energy-efficient lighting, and non-toxic, non-allergenic and locally-sourced building materials, Bardessono is also LEED Platinum certified, honoring a legendary wine country where being green is perfectly natural.

A: Guest study   B: Guest private courtyard
C: Guest bedroom   D: Guest bath
E: Communal courtyard   F: Main lobby
G: Dining   H: Exterior with reflecting pool
Photography: *Sammy Dyess*

WATG   Shangri-La's Villingili Resort & Spa | Villingili Island, Maldives

Shangri-La's Villingili Resort & Spa effortlessly balances modernity, offering state-of-the-art technology and service, with the indigenous flora and fauna on and around Villingili Island, one of nearly 1,200 islands and islets in the 26 atolls of the Maldives, one of Asia's smallest countries in population and land area. The world-class resort features architecture designed by WATG to create three distinctive villages, Lost Horizon, Whispering Palms and Windance, that capture the uniqueness of their sites. Consequently, guests can indulge themselves in a self-contained world of 142 villas on white-sand beaches, a village center with retail, bakery, restaurants and lounges, pool-side barbecue and pool bar, juice bar, ballroom, meeting rooms, karaoke rooms, spa, fitness center, tennis courts, pools, sea sports and diving center, wedding chapel and kids club—long before exploring five neighboring islands. Constructed of wood and stone with thatched roofs, the award-winning resort and spa blend so seamlessly with the lush tropical landscape that indoors and outdoors become almost indistinguishable. As for the villas, incorporating Indian and Middle Eastern motifs, they establish a timeless serenity through flowing, open spaces, abundant scenic views and daylight, soaring ceilings and continuous access to water, attaining a genuine Shangri-La in the Maldives.

A: Villa bedroom   B: Poolside barbeque and pool bar   C: Villas configured as tree houses   D: Infinity pool and villa   E: Villa living room and master bedroom   F: View from villa to ocean
Photography: *Markus Gortz*

A

WATG   The Ritz-Carlton | Guangzhou, China

Strategically located across and down the Pearl River from the new Guangzhou International Convention and Exhibition Center, adjacent to the Guangzhou Opera House and Guangdong National Museum, and steps away from high-end commercial buildings, the new Ritz-Carlton, Guangzhou was designed with bold, contemporary architecture by WATG to serve elite business and leisure travelers. The striking, 42-story structure, accommodating 120 serviced apartments on its lower levels and 351 guestrooms starting on the 20th floor, provides numerous facilities for conducting business and enjoying the best of Guangzhou, a major trading port, commercial center and home to over 10 million people. Besides enjoying guestrooms featuring luxurious materials, fine furnishings and state-of-the-art technology, guests have convenient access to a 6,975-square-foot grand ballroom divisible into three salons, over 11,000 square feet of meeting and conference space, 4,590 square

feet of pre-function space, three multi-functional meeting rooms, two boardrooms, and 24-hour business center, along with such amenities as a monumental lobby lounge, six restaurants and lounges, spa and fitness center with indoor pool, outdoor heated pool, 24-hour gymnasium and yoga room, beauty salon and Ritz-Carlton shop. Known

for setting the standard in hospitality wherever it operates, the Ritz-Carlton has promptly won acclaim in Guangzhou.

A: Registration   B: Outdoor pool   C: Café
D: Porte-cochère   E: Tower
Photography: *Courtesy of Ritz-Carlton, Guangzhou; Paul Dingman*

WATG   The St. Regis Princeville Resort | Princeville, Kaua'i, Hawaii

One of the world's most breathtaking destinations now has a luxury hotel to showcase, the new St. Regis Princeville Resort, overlooking Hanalei Bay on Kauai's exclusive North Shore in Princeville, Hawaii. Designed by WATG in association with Group 70, the St. Regis Princeville brings the St. Regis brand to the Aloha State by transforming an existing facility to introduce 252 magnificent guest rooms, including 51 premium ocean view suites, elegant Halele'a Spa, Prince and Makai champion golf courses, designed by Robert Trent Jones II, and

Kaua'i Grill from renowned chef Jean-Georges Vongerichten, along with a grand lobby, four additional restaurants, 12 meeting and conference rooms, beauty salon, and infinity pool. The design embraces the Hawaiian concept of Ahupua'a, living in balance with nature, by combining Hawaiian art, decorative motifs and colors with high-end appointments incorporating such timeless and frequently native materials as teak, Koa and coconut woods, bronze, limestone, leather, woven raffia, linen, and mother-of-pearl to produce an

atmosphere of luxurious comfort with a Hawaiian residential feel. Surrounded by five majestic mountains, thriving taro farms, a wildlife refuge, equestrian paths, hiking trails, and ancient sea caves and lagoons, the new St. Regis clearly belongs in Hanalei Bay.

*A: Makana Terrace Restaurant **B:** Halele'a Spa **C:** Guestroom **D:** Grand lobby **E:** Porte cochere **F:** Kaua'i Grill*
Photography: *Mark Silverstein, Bruce Buck*

Famed for its history, mythology and Minoan palaces, the Greek island of Crete recently burnished its legendary status when an existing three-star hotel in Rethymnon, in the heart of the Cretan Riviera, emerged from an all-encompassing winter renovation as Grecotel's five-star Creta Palace Hotel, in time for its next summer season. The ambitious facelift, designed by WATG, gives the Creta Palace 355 new guestrooms, suites, bungalows and villas accompanied by new or remodeled arrival and entry areas, lounges, terraces, indoor and outdoor pools, private pools, spa, conference facilities, children's facilities, bars and restaurants. Thanks to a fresh vision for the hotel, creating a sunny, outdoor-oriented and luxurious environment with unique new design strategies, features, finishes and furnishings, the existing main building and three bungalow villages of a popular and much loved establishment have become a distinguished luxury resort. The project's impact can be easily appreciated in guest accommodations, which offer lodging for experiences ranging from family village life to sheer beachfront luxury. In every instance, spaces are infused with natural light and views, the sparkling color palette of Crete, and a rich assortment of materials, finishes and furnishings that graciously complement Creta Palace's splendid sandy beach and hilly terrain.

A: Deluxe 1-Bedroom Bungalow   B: Dream Villa with private pool   C: Indoor and outdoor lobby, lounges and Talos Bar   D: Talos Lounge Bar   E: Family bungalow Suite   F: Palace Luxury Suite   G: Deluxe 1-Bedroom Bungalow Suite with Private Pool   H: Sparkling Lobby Lounge
Photography: *Heinz Troll*

E

F

In the heart of Rovinj, Croatia, an old Istrian town on the Mediterranean Sea dominated by the luminous Baroque Church of St. Euphemia at the summit of its hilltops, the new, 113-room (99 guestrooms, 14 suites) Hotel Monte Mulini is winning the praise of travelers worldwide. A critical factor in the appeal of the five-star luxury resort, designed by WATG, is its distinctive environment. The Monte Mulini's architecture and interiors combine the essence of the Istria lifestyle, a fusion of Italian and Croatian cultures, with contemporary high-end hospitality.

Working closely with the client, Adris Grupa, WATG developed a design with cool, open spaces and floor-to-ceiling glass spread over four levels on a hillside. Guests are thus treated to a spectacular view of the sea from the lobby's panoramic glass wall, warm and inviting bars, lounges and restaurants, a three-level wellness center and spa, and a pool deck featuring four outdoor pools and pool bar, along with guestrooms and suites that feature floor-to-ceiling windows, flat-screen TVs and wi-fi in beautifully appointed, residential-style settings.

Damier Vandelić, Adris Grupa's investments director, notes, "WATG, from my perspective, provides tremendous value to business with their excellent understanding of the value creation process."

A: Exterior from pool deck B: Guestroom terrace C: Restaurant D: Guestroom E: Aerial view F: Spa G: Bar **Photography:** *Renco Koshinozić, Mario Romulić*

G

Every traveler has a personal destination in mind for escaping everyday life, but resisting the charms of the new Four Seasons Resort Mauritius at Anahita, in Anahita, Mauritius, would surely tax anyone's resolve. The 432-acre, golf-oriented development, designed by WATG, features a 123-room, five-star hotel, 36 luxury villas, specialty restaurant, golf course, golf clubhouse, beach club, health spa, spa pavilions, island and lagoon pools, water features and mangrove boardwalk, all seductively arranged as a self-contained community on a private island, Ile au Chats. Planned to allow guests of all ages enjoy a wide array of activities, from recreation, dining, shopping and entertainment to ecological interaction and education, the resort pays homage to the culture and natural life of

Mauritius, a multi-cultural (Hindu, Chinese, Creole, European and Muslim) nation occupying an ancient volcanic island in the Indian Ocean east of Madagascar. Its pavilions, villas and public areas are characterized by stone walls, wooden decks and thatched roofs interspersed with palm trees and tropical gardens, with interiors appointed in the finest quality materials, finishes and furnishings, obtained locally whenever possible but always embracing the latest principles of sustainability. Remote as it may be, the resort appears in Condé Nast Traveler's "Hot List."

A: Restaurant pavilion B: Guest bedroom
C: Villa living room D: Villa bedroom
E: Villa bath F: Pool G: Bar in beach club
Photography: *Paul Thusbaert, Markus Gortz*

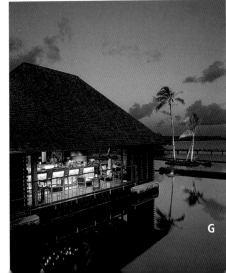

WATG   Halekulani Hotel Renovation | Honolulu, Hawaii

How do you update a legendary Honolulu hotel on Waikiki Beach? The recent renovation of the Halekulani Hotel, designed by WATG, shows what creativity and respect can do for a 453-room luxury resort founded in 1907 and consisting of five, low-density buildings between two and 17 stories high—including the historic, plantation-style Main Building erected in the 1930s—on five acres of lush gardens. In establishing a fresh look for the main lobby, open-air gatehouse, fitness center, hospitality suite, business center, executive board room, Kalia & Kiawe function rooms, ballroom, prefunction living room (in the Main Building), and producing the new, 2,365-square-foot Orchid Suite, WATG has introduced design concepts that remain in harmony with the hotel's existing signature motifs. For example, along with custom-designed furniture keyed to the hotel's unique appearance, WATG includes such special touches as a color scheme rich in amber tones with burgundy accents, Fortuny fabric pillows, a hand-crafted curio showcasing a beautiful shell collection, refurbished original Irene McGowan-designed lighting fixtures, and a custom hand-blown crystal chandelier above a two-story staircase to return aging rooms to their former glory. Describing the outcome, *HiLuxury* comments, "There's a sense of beauty that makes people not want to let go."

A: Exterior of Orchid Suite (ground level)
B: Orchid Suite terrace room   C: Orchid Suite entertainment lounge   D: Orchid Suite master bedroom and bath
Photography: *Barbara Kraft, Ric Noyle/ Courtesy of Hotels & Resorts of Halekulani*

THOMAS SCHOOS

Sustainable Textiles For Hospitality Worldwide

In a FRESH world . . . fabrics live forever.

Index by Project